Resolving Resistance in Group Psychotherapy

Resolving Resistance in Group Psychotherapy

by Leslie Rosenthal, Ph.D.

Jason Aronson Inc.
Northvale, New Jersey
London

THE MASTER WORK SERIES

First softcover edition 1994

Library of Congress Cataloging-in-Publication Data

Rosenthal, Leslie.
  Resolving resistance in group psychotherapy.

  Bibliography: p.
  Includes index.
  1. Group psychotherapy. 2. Resistance (Psycho-
analysis) 3. Psychotherapist and patient. I. Title.
[DNLM: 1. Physician–Patient Relations. 2. Psycho-
therapy, Group. WM 430 R8178r]
RC488.R68 1987   616.89′152   85-19940
ISBN 1-56821-193-7 (softcover)

Manufactured in the United States of America. Jason Aronson Inc. offers books and cassettes. For information and catalog write to Jason Aronson Inc., 230 Livingston Street, Northvale, New Jersey 07647.

Contents

Foreword

Group psychotherapy is part of the psychiatric revolution initiated in 1880 by the psychotherapeutic treatment of Anna O., and it subsequently developed into the system of psychoanalysis organized by Freud and was responsible for great contributions toward the successful handling of the psychoneuroses. With the expansion of the psychotherapeutic armamentarium came increasing demand for psychotherapeutic treatment of larger segments of the population. As described by Dr. Rosenthal in this book, group therapy was discovered, initiated, and has been applied to this ever-widening population. It has proven to be in itself a successful form of psychotherapy. Dr. Rosenthal has been associated with its development for more than a quarter of a century. In this volume he has summarized and integrated the concepts and the experiences he has learned and worked with as a student, teacher, and psychotherapist.

A scientific form of psychotherapy requires a theory and a method of application. The discovery of the concept of resistance has been clearly described. Freud recognized resistance and recommended intelligence as the best method against it.

How intelligence, via interpretation, was applied to overcome resistance has been reported by many authors. In the first chapter of this book, Dr. Rosenthal outlines the newer methods of dealing with resistance, such as: ego reinforcement, mirroring, the use of resistance as a means of communication, and the principle of resolving resistance rather than overcoming it.

How the concept of resistance was applied to the field of group psychotherapy makes a fascinating story. In turn, its recognition and application led to the discovery of counterresistance. The group situation facilitated the handling of resistance and counterresistance and made it possible not only to treat behavior disorders and psychoneuroses but also character disorders, psychosomatic disorders, pre- and postpsychotic states, and the psychoses themselves. It became clear that the emotional state of the therapist was a limiting factor in the successful treatment of these patients. The advent of group psychotherapy, group analysis, individual psychotherapy, individual psychoanalysis, and combined treatment with all these modalities aided the treatment of all patients with psychologically reversible conditions. In addition, the emotional problems and the counterresistances were greatly assisted by the group therapeutic process. Problems encountered in successful treatment were relatively easily resolved, and all individuals involved in the therapeutic process were opened to and yielded to the therapeutic resolution of emotional factors upholding resistance.

The recognition that the group process can help emotional maturation led to the formulation of increasingly specific methods for dealing with therapeutic situations. The differences of opinion about the value of treating individuals as individuals and treating groups as groups developed. Eventually it became clear that specific situations required specific interventions. The problem of the depths of transference and its significance for therapeutic achievement came into focus. Many illustrations have been presented to indicate that all forms of transference occur in groups, as well as in individual treatment, and the success of its management depends on all persons involved.

The therapeutic process came into more detailed study. Many experiences with patients led to the realization that patients and groups function on many different levels. Each level requires a specific theoretical understanding, a specific intellectual and emotional intervention. With the realization that the treatment of individuals was greatly aided by the group therapeutic process, it became important to develop concepts and treatment methods to help the group as a whole. Thus it came to be recognized that not only was the group a place where individuals could be helped but that many people could be helped simultaneously, with great economic and maturational value. It has been observed that there are many different methods of dealing with group members at the same time. Problems of aggression, hostility, and anger can be managed by the way groups are selected, screened, and introduced into the group situation. For the benefit of beginning group therapists, careful selection of patients becomes important. In addition, the use of a co-therapist would be of considerable value. There are many factors that can influence problems of group management. These factors can be controlled to either demobilize or mobilize intense emotional experiences in the group situation.

The experience of psychotherapy has the unexpected effect that the administrator of the therapeutic instrument becomes emotionally involved in the therapeutic process. Many therapists conducting individual and group treatment discover, to their surprise, that they are deeply involved in the process. At first this involvement was regarded as undesirable. Later it came to be recognized that the involvement carried a message that had to be deciphered for therapeutic results. The message had two aspects. On the one hand it might reveal emotional experiences patients may have had with their parents. On the other hand it might reveal previously unknown aspects of the emotional history of the group therapist. Whichever aspect is operating, it is the task of the therapist to recognize both aspects and not let them interfere with his contribution to the therapeutic process.

The book's voluminous bibliography attests to the author's

scholarship, and its well-integrated chapter introductions give testimony to Dr. Rosenthal's mastery of the field of individual and group psychotherapy. By making this book available to students and practitioners in the field of mental health, he has provided an incalculable service. He has laid the foundation for the understanding of the evolution of the field of psychotherapy and has made it possible to continue to participate in the development of the various psychotherapeutic methods, that is, individual therapy, individual psychoanalysis, group therapy, and group psychoanalysis. With the help of the foundation that Dr. Rosenthal has provided us, we can look forward to many new developments. We are beginning to understand forces that make for creative emotional evolution. We are beginning to see that there are advantages and disadvantages in the use of all the psychotherapeutic instruments available. As yet the devastating power of large groups and the channeling of this power into socially constructive forces require much further human endeavor.

Hyman Spotnitz, M.D., Med. Sc.D.

Acknowledgments

A number of people have made important contributions to the emotional and intellectual development that led to this book. S. R. Slavson, a towering figure in group psychotherapy, guided me in my first exposure to the healing powers of the group at the Jewish Board of Guardians. Dr. Hyman Spotnitz imparted the understanding of the protective and communicative functions of resistance and provided constant support for the emotional development requisite to becoming a group analyst. Lia Knopfmacher and Yonata Feldman, both great teachers, contributed richly to my understanding of the uniqueness of the individual. Leo Nagelberg, a friend and colleague, and I had an ongoing exchange of ideas and experiences with transference and resistance that did much to integrate my grasp of these concepts.

I am deeply grateful to my wife, Renee Rosenthal, for her loving determination that this book be written and for her many valuable suggestions that enhanced its clarity and coherence. My children, Regina Granat and her husband Charles,

David, and Alice, have provided rich emotional support and have helped me become a better therapist.

I am much indebted to the members of my groups, my supervisees, and students, who patiently taught me much of what is contained in this book.

Special thanks are due Joan Langs, my editor at Jason Aronson, for her confidence in this work and for her many helpful suggestions as to form, content, and structure.

The Center for Modern Psychoanalytic Studies has for the last 17 years provided a professional home, a sense of belonging and affiliation, and the opportunity to share these ideas with students and colleagues.

Dr. Leslie Rosenthal

12-28-83

To Dave
In long friend-
ship —
Les

Resolving Resistance in
Group Psychotherapy

CHAPTER 1

Resistance in Individual Psychotherapy

A strange and disturbing phenomenon is inevitably encountered by all who work in the field of psychotherapy for reparative change and the alleviation of pain and suffering: A force in the patient emerges to encounter, block, and vitiate the therapeutic endeavors. This universally experienced therapeutic event is called *resistance*; which Dr. William Menninger (1958) defined succinctly as "the trend of forces within the individual which oppose the process of ameliorative change."

The ubiquitous nature of resistance was described by Freud (1912): "Every step of the treatment is accompanied by resistance; every single thought, every mental act of the patient's, must pay toll to the resistance and represents a compromise between the forces urging toward cure and those gathered to oppose it" (p. 210).

Focusing on the centrality of resistance, Menninger identified it as one of Freud's greatest discoveries.

Greenson (1967) also attested to the singular importance of resistance and noted that Freud's discovery of the importance

of analyzing resistance ushered in the beginning of psychoanalysis.

> The concept of resistance is of basic significance for
> psychoanalytic technique and its ramifications touch upon
> every important technical issue. Resistance opposes the
> analytic procedure, the analyst and the patient's reason-
> able ego. Resistance defends the neurosis, the old, the
> familiar, and the infantile from exposure and change.
> [pp. 75–76]

THE DISCOVERY OF RESISTANCE

From 1880 to 1882 Joseph Breuer, a Viennese physician, treated
a young girl suffering from hysteria and obtained considerable
improvement in her symptoms. Breuer treated his young
patient, Anna O., by placing her under hypnosis and eliciting
memories of the circumstances under which her symptoms had
arisen. In the course of this so-called "cathartic method," he
discovered the girl's symptoms disappeared when she recalled
and verbally expressed the precipitating events and her repressed feelings. The patient herself designated this treatment
"the talking cure."

Breuer communicated his experiences and theories to his
younger friend and colleague, Sigmund Freud, who was then
struggling to find an effective treatment for the problem of
neurosis. From Breuer, Freud learned an essential fact about
hysteria: The release of repressed emotion (abreaction) and
making conscious what had been unconscious have demon-
strable therapeutic results. At the time of this exposure to
Breuer's treatment of Anna O., Freud's only treatment tools
were electrotherapy and hypnosis. Freud urged Breuer to
continue with his exploration into this form of treatment of
hysteria, but the latter, a successful general practitioner, had no
desire to delve more deeply into the problems of neurosis.
Breuer finally agreed to publish his findings in conjunction
with Freud, who had begun to use the cathartic method in his

own work. It is in this book, *Studies on Hysteria* (Breuer and Freud 1893–1895), that the first mention of the concept of resistance is found.

In discussing the case of Elizabeth von R., Freud noted how her associations flowed easily at times, with dynamic themes succeeding each other in chronological sequence. He then observed that at other times she manifested inhibition of (then) unknown origin, was unresponsive to the application of pressure, and declared that nothing came to her mind.

Freud conjectured that the patient's silence held in check feelings of self-criticism about her thoughts and wishes to avoid further disagreeable feelings. He then followed with the statement that contains the first mention of resistance (Breuer and Freud 1893–1895): "During this difficult period, I began to attach a profounder significance to the resistance which the patient showed in the reproduction of her recollections and I carefully noted those occasions in which it was especially striking" (p. 110).

Freud goes on to note that some patients were not amenable to hypnosis, and these he would urge to produce memories. "As this urging necessitated much exertion on my part and showed me that I had to overcome a resistance, I therefore formulated the following: Through my psychic work I had to overcome a psychic force in the patient which opposed the pathogenic idea from becoming conscious" (p. 200).

Freud described the process of repression as a "force of repulsion against an unbearable idea entering the patient's ego" (p. 201). He observed that when he sought to direct the patient's attention to it, he encountered this force as a "resistance" to the patient's recalling the genesis of the symptom. In this context, Freud acknowledges that urging and persuasion by an inexperienced physician do not suffice to overcome "association resistance" in a severe case of hysteria (p. 202).

In Chapter 4 of *Studies on Hysteria*, "The Psychotherapy of Hysteria," Freud gives a detailed description of the resistances encountered. It should be noted that, as part of his technique, he would press his hands against the patient's head as a means of helping him produce memories.

Thus far I have warmly praised the achievements of pressure procedure and have entirely neglected the aspect of the defense or the resistance, so that I certainly must have given the impression that by means of a small artifice one is placed in a position to become master of the psychic resistances to the cathartic method. But to believe this would be a gross mistake. The pressure procedure is nothing but a trick serving to surprise for a while the defensive ego; in all graver cases it soon recalls its intentions and continues its resistance. [p. 210]

Freud then continues with a passage that succinctly conveys his realization of the inevitability of resistance. Despite the patient's good will and conscious wishes to cooperate, he cannot keep to the terms of the agreement:

It is remarkable how completely the patients—even the most tractable and the most intelligent—forget the agreement into which they have previously entered. They have promised to tell everything that occurs to them, be it intimately related to them or not, be it agreeable to say or not; that is, they are to tell everything without any choice, or influence of criticism or affect. Yet, they do not keep their promise, it is apparently beyond their powers. The work repeatedly stops, they continue to assert that this time nothing came to their mind. [p. 210]

Freud goes on to describe some of the subterfuges by which the resistances are cloaked: "I am distracted today, the clock disturbs me." Or, the patient seeks to disavow his recollections with remarks such as, "Something occurred to me, but only because you talked it into me."

Studies on Hysteria, generally considered to be the first important document in the history of psychoanalysis, also gives the first exposition of technique for handling resistance. In the face of patients' assertions that nothing comes to their minds, Freud offers: "One need not believe them, and one must always assume, and also say, that they hold back something because they believe it to be unimportant or perceive it as painful. One must insist, and assume an assured attitude until one really hears something" (p. 210).

When faced with evasions by the patient or attempts to avoid responsibility for his utterances, Freud indicates that "in all these cases I remain inflexibly firm, I admit none of these distractions, but I explain to the patient that these are only forms and subterfuges of the resistance" (p. 211). He recommends that the analyst keep watching the patient for facial expressions that help distinguish a genuine nonappearance of a memory from the patient's attempts to disavow or repel an emerging thought. Freud indicates that this helps in gleaning clues as to which direction to investigate and "what things we have to force upon the patient. For some cases this suffices, for it essentially is a question of finding the secret, and telling it to the patient, so that he is then usually forced to relinquish his resistance" (p. 212).

In *Studies on Hysteria* Freud offers this summation of his technique for dealing with resistance:

> What means have we now at our disposal to overcome the continued resistance? Few, but they include almost all those by which one man can ordinarily exert a psychical influence on another. In the first place we must remember that psychic resistance, especially one of long continuance, can only be broken slowly and with much patience. In the next place, we may reckon on the intellectual interest which the patient begins to feel after working in analysis for a brief period. On explaining and imparting to him the knowledge of the marvelous world of psychic processes, we obtain his collaboration and cause him to view himself with the objective interest of the investigator. But finally—and this remains the strongest motive force— we must endeavor, after we have discovered the motives for his defense, to deprive them of their value and strength or even replace them by stronger ones. One does as well as he can as an explainer (where ignorance has produced shyness), as a teacher, as a representative of a

freer and superior philosophy of life, and as a confessor, who through the continuance of his sympathy and respect, imparts absolution, as it were, after the confession. One endeavors to do something humane for the patient as far as the range of one's own personality and the measure of sympathy which one can set apart for the case allows. [p. 213]

Thus, in *Studies on Hysteria*, the term *resistance* is introduced and some preliminary formulations are offered. One had to overcome a psychical force in the patient that was opposed to pathogenic ideas, painful thoughts, and memories. The patient's ego created a defense—a force that repelled the disturbing idea from the consciousness and opposed its return in memory. Resistance was therefore originally defined in psychoanalytic theory as action taken by the ego to protect the process of repression. When the patient and analyst attempted to bring pathogenic ideas into consciousness, resistance was an interfering force.

It is the task of the analyst, Freud states, to overcome this resistance. He does this by a variety of techniques: He applies pressure to the forehead; he insists that memories will be forthcoming; he urges, explains, and shows inflexible firmness in the face of subterfuge, denial, and avoidance by the patient; he "forces things upon the patient." He learns the secret the patient is seeking to withhold, and by telling it to the patient (interpreting), forces him to relinquish his resistance. He enlists the patient's intellectual interest in his own psychology. He teaches, elucidates, presents himself as an example of emotional health. He absolves through confession with respect and sympathy for the patient.

In an 1897 letter to his friend Wilheim Fleiss, Freud wrote: "An idea about resistance has enabled me to put back on the rails the cases of mine which looked like breaking down. Resistance, which is in the last resort the thing that stands in the way of the work, is nothing but the child's character" (p. 226). In this brief reference lay the first clue that resistance was an immature method of functioning, an idea that foreshadowed subsequent developments in the perception and comprehension of resistance.

In *The Interpretation of Dreams* (1900), Freud made various references to the concept of resistance, at times speaking of censorship in dreams as being due to resistance or being imposed by resistance. Thus, after discussing the interplay of the mechanism of displacement, distortion, and overdetermination in dreams, Freud notes "a second condition which must be satisfied by those elements of the dream thoughts which make their way into dreams: *they must escape the censorship imposed by resistance*" (Freud 1900, p. 308). At another point Freud sees a form of condensation in the dream, in which a composite person is created from two persons who share a common feeling. He notes:

It is easy to see how well this method of representation can serve to evade the censorship due to resistance, which imposes such severe conditions upon the dream-work. What the censorship objects to may be precisely uncertain ideas which, in the material of the dream-thoughts, are attached to a particular person; do I proceed to find a second person, who is also connected with the objectionable material, but only with part of it. The figure arrived at by composition may then be admissable to the dream-contact without censorship. [pp. 321–322]

Freud suggests that the concepts of resistance and censorship are closely related to each other, with censorship being related to dreams as resistance is to free association. In this context, Freud says of the forgetting of dreams:

I am in a position to offer a demonstration of the fact that the forgetting of dreams is, to a great extent, a product of resistance. One of my patients will tell me he has had a dream but has forgotten every trace of it. We proceed with our work. I come up against a resistance; I therefore explain something to the patient and help him by encouragement and pressure to come to terms with some disagreeable thought. Hardly have I succeeded in this than he exclaims: "Now I remember what it was I dreamt." The same resistance which interfered with our work that day also made him forget the dream. By overcoming the resistance I have recalled a dream to his memory. [p. 520]

Freud points out the patient's uncertainty and doubt concerning the accuracy of a dream or of individual data of the dream. "This resistance has not yet exhausted itself by the displacements and substitutions which it has effected, so that it still clings in the form of doubt as to what has been allowed to emerge" (p. 516). In discussing the meaning of doubt in the reporting of a dream, Freud made the often quoted statement: "Whatever interrupts the progress of the analytic work is a resistance" (p. 517). This is obviously a wider concept of resistance than a concept primarily connected with repressed memories.

Freud's Psycho-Analytic Method (1904) contains the earliest definitive declaration that the factor of resistance had become one of the cornerstones of his theory. In this paper Freud describes his psychoanalytic procedure as an outgrowth of the cathartic method reported on by himself and Breuer in *Studies on Hysteria*. He reports the shedding of hypnosis as a therapeutic tool and its replacement by the method of free association. Freud notes that when patients are asked to give a detailed account of their case histories, there are invariably amnesias of some kind. When urged to fill in these memory gaps, the thoughts that occur to them are pushed back. If memories are recovered, patients evince actual discomfort.

Freud concludes from this experience that the amnesias are the result of a process he calls *repression*, the motivation for which he finds in feelings of pain. The psychical forces that have brought about this repression are traceable to resistance, which operates against the reintegration of these memories.

The factor of resistance has become one of the cornerstones of Freud's theory. He regards the ideas pushed aside with excuses as derivatives of the repressed psychical manifestations (thoughts and impulses), and as distortions of these due to the resistance that is exerted against their reproduction. "The greater the resistance the greater the distortion" (Freud 1904, p. 251).

Freud explains his abandonment of hypnosis on the basis that it concealed the resistance, "and for this reason has obstructed the physician's insight into the play of psychic forces. Hypnosis does not do away with resistance but only avoids it and therefore yields only incomplete information and transitory therapeutic success" (p. 253).

At this point, resistance has come to assume an important place in Freud's theory of psychoanalysis. However, it is still connected with the defense of repression, since lifting the amnesias continued to be the goal of treatment. The attachment of resistance to repression is clear. In this paper on his psychoanalytic method, Freud (1904) wrote:

> The task of the treatment is to remove the amnesias. When all gaps in memory have been filled in, all the enigmatic products of mental life elucidated, the continuance and even a renewal of the morbid condition are made impossible. The formula may be expressed in this fashion: all repressions must be undone. Another formulation reaches further: the task consists in making the unconscious accessible to consciousness, which is done by overcoming the resistances. [p. 92]

In the case of Dora in *Fragment of an Analysis of a Case of Hysteria* (1905), Freud illustrated how the transference of Dora's revengeful feelings toward a betraying lover onto Freud, himself, became the most powerful source of resistance in the case. Her acting out of this transference resistance led to the patient breaking off analysis. In his discussion of the case, Freud states:

> The transference took me unawares, and because of the unknown quantity in me which reminded Dora of Herr K, she took her revenge on him and deserted me as she believed herself to have been deserted by him. Thus, she

acted an essential part of her recollection and phantasies instead of reproducing it in the treatment. When it is possible to work transferences into the analysis at an early stage, the course of the analysis is retarded and obscured, but its existence is better guaranteed against sudden and overwhelming resistance. [p. 118]

As noted previously, when Freud first recognized the existence of resistance as a clinical phenomenon, his method of dealing with it was based on his current conception that a cure consisted of the lifting of amnesia and the unearthing of pathological ideas that had been repelled from conscious awareness. He sought to circumvent and overcome the resistance to free association by "psychical compulsion," to gain direct access to the memories. However, this pressuring approach proved to have negative effects on some patients and led Freud to gradually address himself primarily to the interfering factors. He began to deal directly with the resistance, which freed the individual to recall and verbalize repressed material. This developing shift in emphasis is reflected in the brief paper *Observations on Wild Analysis* (Freud 1910): "The pathological factor is not the patient's ignorance in itself, but the root of the ignorance in his inner resistances; it was they that first called this ignorance into being, and they still maintain it now. In combating these resistances lies the task of therapy" (p. 302).

TRANSFERENCE RESISTANCE

In *The Dynamics of Transference* (1912), Freud clearly locates the transference relationship of patient to analyst as "the site of the strongest resistance to the cure" and "the most formidable ally of the resistance" (p. 101). Going beyond merely stating that transference causes the most powerful resistances, Freud explains the dynamic forces involved in the mobilization of this resistance against the analytic work. He also distinguishes between positive and negative transference and suggests that the transference to the analyst provides the foundation for resistance, insofar as it consists of negative (hostile) feelings or repressed, erotic elements that underlie the positive feelings.

In *On Beginning the Treatment* (1913), Freud identifies some initial resistances that patients may raise. These include planned and prepared communications, which are ostensibly introduced to make more efficient use of the analytic hour but are actually employed to guard against the appearance of unwelcome thoughts. Another type of resistance is dilution of the treatment through discussion of the treatment with others.

In the next in his series of papers on technique, *Remembering, Repeating and Working Through* (1914), Freud begins with a succinct review of changes in psychoanalytic technique. These changes reflect profound modifications in psychoanalysis' approach to and use of resistance. Its first phase was that of Breuer's catharsis, which involved concentration upon the events producing symptoms. The aims pursued, with the help of hypnosis, were recollection and abreaction. In the second phase, hypnosis was abandoned and the main task became deriving from the patient's free associations what he failed to remember. There was still a major emphasis on the situation that spawned the illness, but abreaction receded in importance and was replaced by the work necessary to overcome the patient's resistance to free association. In the final phase, the analyst abandons concentration on any particular problem, studies whatever is occupying the patient's mind at the moment, and uses interpretation mainly for the purpose of dealing with resistances as they emerge.

In this paper Freud first mentions a special category of resistance: the repetition compulsion. This is the need to repeat and reenact past experience, instead of remembering it. "We may say that the patient *remembers* nothing of what is forgotten and repressed but that he expresses it in *action*. He reproduces it not in his memory but in his behavior; he repeats it without of course knowing that he is repeating it" (Freud 1914, p. 149). Freud notes that the stronger the resistance, the more extensively will repetition and reenactment be substituted for remembering. "The resistances determine the succession of the various repetitions. The past is the patient's armoury out of which he fetches his weapons for defending himself against the progress of the analysis, weapons which we must wrest from him" (p. 150). Freud indicates that these resistances are especially tenacious and require "working through."

> One must allow the patient time to get to know this resistance of which he is ignored, to "work through" it, to overcome it by continuing the work according to the analytic rule. Only when it has come to its height can one discover the repressed instinctual trends which are feeding this resistance. [p. 150]

The importance of this process is emphasized by Freud, who states:

> This working through of the resistances may in practice amount to an arduous task for the patient and a trial of patience for the analyst. Nevertheless, it is the part of the work that effects the greatest changes in the patient and that distinguishes analytic treatment from every kind of suggestive treatment. [p. 151]

In his third paper on technique, *Observations on Transference Love* (1915), Freud discusses the resistive aspects of the "love transference," in which the patient falls in love with the analyst. He refers to the patient's efforts to "reassure herself of her irresistibility, to destroy the physician's authority by bringing him down to the level of a lover and to gain all the other advantages which she foresees as incidental to the gratification of her love" (p. 38). Freud also notes that the patient's declarations of love are a trap set by her resistance to lure the analyst into a compliance that would leave him open to her criticism. He continues: "But above all one obtains the impression that the resistance acts as an agent provocateur, intensifying the love of the patient and exaggerating her readiness for sexual surrender, in order to vindicate the action of her repression more emphatically by pointing to the dangers of such licentiousness" (p. 381). He concludes:

> She is bringing out a resistance, therefore under the guise of being in love, and in addition to this she has no compunction about trying to lead him into a cleft stick. For if he refuses her love, as duty and understanding compel him to do, she can take up the attitude that she has been humiliated and, out of revenge, make herself inaccessible to cure by him, just as she is now doing ostensibly out of love. [p. 386]

In *Introductory Lectures on Psychoanalysis* (1915–1917), Freud first refers to resistance in his lecture on the manifest and latent elements in dreams. In analysis an "inviolable rule" is laid down that the patient must not hold back any idea or thought, even if he finds it too unimportant, too senseless, irrelevant, or too distressing. "The dreamer promises to obey the rule, and we may be annoyed afterward to find how badly he keeps his promise when the occasion arises" (p. 115). Freud continues:

> We perceive that the work of interpreting dreams is carried out in the face of a *resistance*, which opposes it and of which the dreamer's critical objections are manifestation. This resistance is something entirely new. The appearance is something entirely new. The appearance of this new factor comes to us as a not altogether pleasant surprise. We suspect that it is not going to make our work any easier. It might mislead us into abandoning our whole concern with dreams: Something so unimportant as a dream and, on top of that, all these difficulties instead of a simple straight-forward technique! But, on the other hand, these difficulties might act precisely as a stimulus and make us suspect that the work will be worth the trouble. We regularly come up against resistance when we try and make our way forward from the substitute which is the dream-element to the unconscious material hidden behind it. So we may conclude that there must be some-

thing of importance concealed behind the substitute. If a child refuses to open his clenched fist to show what he has in it, we may feel sure that it is something wrong— something he ought not to have. [p. 116]

In his nineteenth lecture, Freud deals fully with resistance:

When we undertake to restore a patient to health, to relieve him of his illness, he meets us with a violent and tenacious resistance, which persists throughout the whole length of treatment. This is such a strange fact that we cannot expect it to find much credence. It is best to say nothing about it to the patient's relatives, for they invariably regard it as an excuse on our part for the length or failure of our treatment. The patient, who is suffering so much from his symptoms and is causing those about him to share his sufferings, who is ready to undertake so many sacrifices in time, money, effort and self-discipline in order to be freed from these symptoms—we are to believe that this same person puts up a struggle in the interest of his illness against the person who is helping him. Yet, it is true; and when its improbability is pointed out to us, we need only reply that it is not without its analogies. A man who has gone to the dentist with an unbearable toothache will nevertheless try to hold the dentist back when he approaches the sick tooth with a pair of forceps. [p. 287]

Freud illustrates some of the maneuvers that patients use to avoid the fundamental rule requiring them to say everything that occurs to them:

At one moment he declares that nothing occurs to him, at the next that so many thoughts are crowding in on him that he cannot get hold of anything. Presently we observe with pained astonishment that he has given way first to one and then to another critical objection; he betrays this to us by the long pauses. He then admits that there is something he really cannot say—he would be ashamed to; and he allows this reason to prevail against his promise. Or he says that something has occurred to him, but it concerns another person not himself and is therefore exempt from being reported. Or, what has now occurred to him is really too unimportant, too silly and senseless. So it goes on with innumerable variations. [p. 288]

Freud also notes the use of "intellectual resistance" by patients who focus on the theory of psychoanalysis and raise all sorts of questions to the analyst:

The patient is willing to be argued with, he is anxious to get us to instruct him, teach him, contradict him, introduce him to the literature, so that he can find further instruction. He is quite ready to become an adherent of psycho-analysis—on condition that analysis spares him personally. [p. 289]

In this lecture Freud refers again to the "transference resistance, the overcoming of which is among the most difficult of technical problems" (p. 290). Freud says these transference resistances communicate valuable information about the patient, so their emergence and appearance are welcome:

Resistances of the kind should not be one-sidedly condemned. They include so much of the most important material from the patient's past and bring it back in so convincing a fashion that they become some of the best supports of the analysis if a skillful technique knows how to give them the right turn. Nevertheless, it remains a remarkable fact that this material is always in the service of the resistance and brings to the fore a *facade* that is hostile to the treatment. Yet, you must not get an impression that we regard these resistances as an unforeseen risk to analytic influence. No, we are aware that these resistances are bound to come to light; in fact we are dissatisfied if we cannot provide them clearly enough and are unable to demonstrate them to the patient. [p. 291]

Freud then makes the famous declaration that so emphatically establishes the centrality of the concept of resistance in psychoanalysis: "Indeed we come finally to understand the overcoming of these resistances is the only part of our work which gives us an assurance that we have achieved something with the patient" (p. 291).

In these *Introductory Lectures* Freud also asserts that the more severe emotional disorders, the narcissistic neuroses, are not amenable to the psychoanalytic method, since such patients have no capacity for transference and show irreversible resistance. He states:

What always happens with them is that after proceeding for a short distance, we come up against a wall which brings us to a stop. In the narcissistic neuroses the resistance is unconquerable, at the most we are able to cast an inquisitive glance over the top of the wall and spy out what is going on on the other side of it. [p. 423]

In *Inhibitions, Symptoms and Anxiety* (1926) Freud sets forth five basic types of resistance according to their source in the dynamic structure of the psyche:

1. Opposition, emanating from the ego, to remembering and verbalizing emotionally significant life history, also called "repressing resistance."
2. Resistance of secondary gain, wherein the ego manipulates to gain whatever special benefits or consideration the individual has been accorded because of his illness.
3. Superego resistance, which is characterized by a sense of guilt or shame and a need for punishment.

4. Repetition-compulsion resistance, which expresses itself in the craving and demand for some form of action, either aggressive or sexual.
5. Transference resistance.

The paper *Analysis Terminable and Interminable* (1937) contains some further formulations of the nature of resistance. Freud suggests that three factors determine the results of treatment: the influence of early trauma, the constitutional strength of the instincts, and alterations of the ego. Freud notes: "The factors which are prejudicial to analysis and may cause it to be so long-drawn out as to be really interminable are a constitutional strength of instinct and an unfavorable modification of the ego in the defensive conflict, a modification comparable to a dislocation or crippling" (p. 224).

DEFENSES AND RESISTANCE

Freud (1937) goes on to describe the process by which the ego, seeking to protect itself against threatening instincts, employs defense mechanisms that weaken it and affect its ability to perceive and cope with reality:

> The psychical apparatus is intolerant of unpleasure and strives to ward it off at all cost and, if the perception of reality involves unpleasure, that perception—the truth—must be sacrificed. The ego's defensive mechanisms are condemned to falsify the inner perception, so that it transmits to us only an imperfect and travestied picture of our id. . . . Not infrequently it turns out that the ego has paid too high a price for the services which these mechanisms render. [p. 244]

Freud continues, "The purpose of the defensive mechanisms is to avert dangers . . . but they produce an ever-growing alienation from the external world and a permanent enfeeblement of the ego" (p. 245). Freud then discusses how these defensive reactions are repeated in the analysis, and states:

The crux of the matter is that the mechanisms of defense against former dangers recur in analysis in the form of resistances to cure but follow that the ego treats recovery itself as a new danger. . . . If the analyst tries to explain to the patient one of the distortions which his defense has produced and to correct it, he meets with a complete lack of comprehension and an imperviousness to valid arguments. We then see that *there really is a* resistance to the discovery of resistances and that the defensive mechanisms do deserve the name we gave them: they are resistances not only to bringing of id-contents into consciousness but also to the whole process of analysis and so to cure. [p. 246]

In this same paper, Freud speculates on factors that might explain why the analytic process is so slow in certain patients. He describes some of these patients as showing a rigidity and lack of mobility in their libido. They seem unable to detach feelings from one object to another, and Freud ascribes this condition to a type of resistance he designates "adhesiveness of the libido" (p. 242). He suggests that these patients—who show such immutable resistance in analysis and cling so tenaciously to illness and suffering—are showing a "resistance of the id" (p. 242) based on a self-destructive sense of guilt derived from the death instinct (p. 243).

GLOVER'S EXTENSIONS

After Freud, the next comprehensive treatment of the concept of resistance was that of Edward Glover (1928), who takes a multifaceted categorizing approach to the problem of "undermining and resolving the defense-resistances" (p. 30).

From the clinical viewpoint, Glover divides resistances into *obvious* and *unobstrusive* varieties, a classification following the histological one of macroscopic and microscopic appearance. Glover observes that the resistances that cause the most trouble are likely to arise unnoticed. Obvious manifestations of resistance may range from slips of the tongue to lateness, absence, silence, and premature termination. He suggests: "The most successful resistances are silent, and it might be said that the sign of their existence is our unawareness of them. Thus, resistances exist which we are able to detect most often in retrospect, and of which we first become aware on account of a slowing of progress" (pp. 30–31).

Glover illustrates this "doldrum resistance" by the patient who seems cooperative, talks of early memories and fantasies, and seems to be progressing satisfactorily until it dawns on the analyst that the treatment has been at a standstill for some time. "It is as if we have been watching under a magnifying glass a piece of radioactive material shedding constant emanations without any obvious diminution of weight" (p. 32). Other examples of unobstructive resistance are a constant preoccupation with emotional material that has little direct connection to the patient's own experience, and a barely perceptible deflection of attention onto nonanalytic subjects.

Glover next addresses resistance at a functional level. He notes that resistance was originally seen exclusively as evidence of the operation of repression, but the notion of repression was found inadequate to embrace all the elements of defense. Repression was then shorn of its bulk and became, along with reaction-formation, regression, and so forth, one of the mechanisms of defense. "But," Glover continues, "it is still true to say that each and all of the mechanisms of defense can function as resistance. However we may approach the mental apparatus, there is no part of its functioning which cannot serve the purposes and hence give rise during analysis to the phenomenon of resistance" (p. 33). Glover observes that defensive processes (resistance) are not simply artifacts of the analytic situation but are always present. He describes the protective functions involved in two defenses, sublimation and rationalization.

Glover's third avenue of approach to resistance is via the transference resistances, "a highly specialized ego-defense, in which an attempt is made to avoid the uncovering of unconscious ideas by their reexperiencing in analysis of the incest-wish and the incest-barrier and the experience of the early Oedipus situation in all its strength and horror" (p. 37). To this is added the emotional voltage of the patient's earlier (preoedipal) wishes and his reactions to thwarting at oral, anal, and phallic levels, with their associated sadistic impulses.

Glover (1928) then considers resistance in relation to fixation points in development and the forms they manifest in different clinical conditions. Thus, repression is the characteristic defense mechanism in hysteria; regression, reaction-formation, reaction-formation undoing, and isolation are the defense mechanisms in obsessional neurosis; introjection is the mechanism in depression; and projection is the mechanism in paranoia. He suggests that this classification can be of help in the analysis of resistance, since it explains the operation and tenacity of certain resistances:

The necessity which the hysteric shows for feverish retention of an inflamed transference-situation makes us understand one of the reasons why the analysis of transference is so vigorously resisted: the patient is struggling to avoid a traumatic situation implied in transference dissolution. [p. 39]

Glover goes on to discuss the "seemingly intractable" id resistances that arise from the compulsion to repeat an earlier gratification. Because of their powerful emotional charge, these resistances seem impervious to interpretation and only succumb to the consistent erosion of the working-through process.

In a reference to those resistances that arise to protect the gratifications derived from the illness, Glover notes that these can be clearly observed at two points in every analysis: first in the course of the developing transference, and later, at the end of analysis when "the patient, apprehending loss of the transference situation or finally realizing that transference demands are barren of fulfillment, endeavors to fall ill once more" (p. 45).

WILHELM REICH: CHARACTER ARMORING

Wilhelm Reich, in his two papers on character formation and character analysis, contributed to the psychoanalytic understanding of resistance. He demonstrated that among the various resistances of patients to analysis were a group of character resistances: habitual attitudes and behavioral reactions that serve as armor against external stimuli and impulses from within.

Continuing with his delineation of character and character resistance, Reich states:

> The character consists in a chronic change of the ego which one might describe as a *hardening*, its purpose is to protect the ego from external and internal dangers. As a protective formation that has become chronic, it merits the designation "armoring" for it clearly constitutes a restriction of the psychic mobility of the personality as a whole. [p. 172]

Reich illustrates the development of a character trait, such as shyness, as a weak ego's defense against forbidden impulses. The shyness represents a transformation of the ego—the development of attitudes designed to ward off fear.

Reich speaks of character armor as "the molded expression of narcissistic defense chronically embedded in the psychic structure" (p. 56). Above and beyond the known resistances that are automatically called into operation to keep unconscious impulses at bay, there is a constant resistive factor rooted in the unconscious and expressed in the total personality rather than in specific symptoms. This is character resistance, and it is expressed in the individual's typical behavior patterns of walking, talking, smiling, ingratiating, flattering, rebelling, and so forth.

In discussing the technique of character (resistance) analysis, Reich offers several suggestions. He says it is necessary to single out the character trait from which the cardinal resistance proceeds and to work it through analytically by interpreting its meaning (Reich 1928).

> In character analysis we have to isolate the character trait and put it before the patient again and again until he has succeeded in breaking clear of it. In breaking clear of and objectifying the neurotic character trait, the patient begins to experience it as something alien to himself. [p. 60]

Reich suggests that every resistance consists of two unconscious impulses: an id impulse that is warded off and an ego impulse that wards off. The analyst gives precedence to that part of the resistance that is closer to the surface—the ego defense. The resistance is thus approached without intrusion into the area of the threatening id impulse. The patient is helped to understand that he is defending against something, then is helped to see *how* he is defending himself. Later in the analysis, when sufficient inroads into the resistance have been attained, the patient is helped to discover *what* he is defending against.

Reich also devotes attention to the general problem of the analysis of resistance. He lays down the principle that the interpretation of resistance should precede the interpretation of content. He stresses the necessity of alertness to the *latent resistances*, "attitudes on the part of the patient which are not expressed directly and immediately, i.e., in the form of doubt, distrust, silence, obstinacy, apathy, etc., but indirectly in the analytic performance" (p. 32). He suggests dealing with the "cardinal resistance" rather than taking up individual peripheral resistances.

Reich notes that the intuitive capacity of the analyst is a significant factor in dealing with resistance. "There are of course no rules for ferreting out the resistances and divining of their contemporary meaning. To a large extent, this is a matter of intuition—and here we have the beginning of the unteachable art of analysis" (p. 33). Reich's highly active approach to resistance is reflected in his axiom that "resistances cannot be taken up soon enough and that apart from the resistances, the interpretation of the unconscious cannot be held back enough" (p. 45).

In his book *Character Analysis* (1933) Reich elaborated on

what he termed "systematic resistance analysis." In this approach, each patient is viewed as inherently resistive, regardless of surface appearances of cooperativeness. In the face of the inevitable negativism of the patient, Reich recommended a therapeutic strategy that focused exclusively on the systematic analysis of resistance.

ANNA FREUD: THE MECHANISMS OF DEFENSE

The next major discussion of resistance was by Anna Freud (1936) in *The Ego and the Mechanisms of Defense*. Freud seeks to systematize an understanding of the various mechanisms of defense and their relation to resistance. In this work she observes that resistances are not only obstacles to the treatment but also important sources of information about the general functioning of the ego.

The data upon which we base our understanding of the ego emerges in the form of resistance to the analysis of the id. The ego is activated in analysis by the inroads of the id. Since it is the aim of the analysis to further these inroads, that is, to facilitate the emergence of unconscious wishes and impulses into consciousness, the ego's defensive operations are automatically set in motion to actively resist the analysis. In addition, since the analyst directly exerts his influence to bring about the emergence of these impulses (through securing the patient's observance of the fundamental rule of free association), the ego's defensive maneuvers take the form of direct opposition and hostility to the analyst himself.

OTTO FENICHEL: THE MANAGEMENT OF RESISTANCE

Fenichel also dealt extensively with the concept of resistance and with interpretive techniques in its management. He noted that by observance of the fundamental rule of analysis, the attempt is made to eliminate (as much as possible) the regulating activity of the ego, so the derivative of the unconscious becomes more clearly recognizable as such. However, Fenichel notes, even when the patient sincerely tries to follow the basic rule of free association, some resistances remain. The patient is not even aware that his ego is still interfering with the free flow of his associations. The analyst can observe the "alternate approaching and receding of the unconscious impulse" and the tenacious effectiveness of the resistance, even when the basic rule is applied.

In the area of technique, Fenichel states that the first correct interpretation to be given may be the simple statement, "You are in a state of resistance." He declares that this interpretation, when presented in a noncritical tone, can make the patient aware of something he has not known previously. "Even if nothing else can be said about a resistance than that it is present, it is certainly better to call the patient's attention to it than to leave it unheeded" (Fenichel 1941, p. 50). In offering guidelines for interpretation, Fenichel confirms Reich's axiom that interpretation of resistance precedes interpretation of content (p. 45):

> An effective interpretation of content succeeds because of a consonance between external auditory perceptions and internally experienced impulses, such a consonance enabling the impulse to break through. A consonance is not possible when it is blocked by a wall of resistance which makes the recognition of the impulse unfeasible. In this case we must first remove the wall. [p. 45]

Fenichel's classical approach to the management of resistance being based exclusively on interpretation is clearly defined. "We must say that we obtain the desired effect upon the patient all the more lastingly if we succeed in using no other means of eliminating resistances than the confrontation of his reasonable ego with the fact of his resistance and the history of its origin" (p. 20).

We find in Fenichel an echo of Freud's statement that

resistance represents the character of the child. "If the analyst does not understand the details of his patient's childhood from the beginning, there is nothing to worry about. The patient's childhood is still present in his behavior today" (p. 49).

Fenichel also addresses the problem of character resistance, "the modes of defense anchored in the character" (p. 66) and, in agreement with Reich, states: "It is particularly urgent that we work first to release the personality from its rigidity because it is in this that the pathogenic energies are really bound. The directing of one's attention to the 'rigid' defenses can be of decisive importance" (p. 66). Fenichel speculates on the factors that cause one patient to produce more of the living transference resistance and another to display more of the rigid character resistances. He suggests: "It depends upon whether the ego banishes anxiety and symptoms from its domain after their first appearance by some further defensive measure (the transference action would then be in the escape discharge), or whether the ego builds the anxiety and symptom into itself, altering its own character" (p. 68). Fenichel then offers a technical rule about character resistances: "In order to attack them successfully, we must first change character resistances into transference resistances exactly in the same well-known way that we first change character neuroses into symptomatic neurosis" (p. 68).

Fenichel describes a number of resistances encountered in analysis. He offers the example of a patient who protects himself against being surprised by his feared feelings through a swift readiness to render interpretations of his own. Another patient was given to describing his feelings as if he were a physician conducting an examination or giving a case history, rather than as a patient experiencing them. A third type of identified resistance is that of a pathological wish for recovery that consists of the patient's magical hopes for the strengthening of his neurotic equilibrium and his infantile wish of fulfillment. Of these patients, Fenichel says, "They do not want from the analysis a liberation from the crutches of their neuroses. They expect stronger crutches" (p. 26). Fenichel notes that the expectation of getting well may, in some cases, function as a resistance when recovery is equated with the gratification of a forbidden impulse.

Theodor Reik (1915) declared: "If anyone were to ask how the patient's resistance expresses itself, the answer would run: in all those hindrances which oppose themselves to the restitution of the patient's health and effective capacity—all the obstacles which the patient puts in the way of his becoming well" (p. 143). Reik illustrates a number of resistances. One is the need to prove the analyst wrong, for example, asking advice and then acting on it in a way that will bring about unfortunate results. "Defiant obedience," offering refusal while slavishly following the analyst's directions, is another form of resistance.

HYMAN SPOTNITZ: RESISTANCE REINFORCEMENT

An innovative approach to resistance and a major emphasis on it developed from the work of Spotnitz and his co-workers at the Child Guidance Institute of the Jewish Board of Guardians in New York City, from the early 1940s through the next decade. Working primarily with ambulatory patients or borderline schizophrenics who were considered poor risks for traditional methods of treatment, Spotnitz evolved the approach of "reinforcement of resistances." This approach was based on an understanding of resistances as instruments necessary for maintaining the patient's emotional equilibrium. This approach was heralded in a report by Spotnitz and colleagues (1957) on the withdrawn child's need for insulation against the overstimulating impact of other people:

They describe a therapeutic interaction in which the therapist joined the child in whatever discussion he initiated. If the child showed interest in cars, inventions, sports, wars, the therapist would start talking about these topics. *As he went along with Samuel's resistiveness* and, so to speak, *took part in it*, the boy's stiffness was replaced by behavior that was more natural for a ten-year-old boy and positive feelings for the therapist emerged. [p. 245]

The same three authors described a technique of psychological mirroring of the child's resistance attempts to evoke a response from the therapist. This process of reflection was designated "ego reinforcement."

These concepts were expanded upon by Spotnitz and Nagelberg (1960) in a later publication:

They note that the type of psychological defense erected by these patients was described by Freud as the "stonewall of narcissism," a defense he regarded as insurmountable. The authors indicate that their investigations tended to demonstrate that the wall could not be overthrown without endangering the personality behind it. They then describe their therapeutic strategy: "In essence, the approach which we delineate constitutes an outflanking of the wall, thus enabling it to stand and continue to fulfill its defensive function until the patient has outgrown the need for its protection and can safely be exposed to the more conventional analytic procedures." [p. 193]

The goal of this intensive psychotherapy is the same as that sought in the psychoanalytic treatment of the neuroses—to resolve the patients' inner resistances to free association. However, these are characteristically dealt with in an entirely different way.

No attempt is made to overcome the resistances through objective interpretation or through pressure on the patient to give them up. On the contrary, the therapist supports and reinforces resistances, he helps to maintain the narcissistic defense. This theoretical approach strongly suggests the old adage: If you can't beat em, join em. [p. 193]

The authors explain that this strategy is dictated by two consistent findings. First, when the narcissistic patient is not pressured to overcome his resistances, he has a diminishing need to maintain them. Second, helping him to retain his resistances until he is capable of mastering and outgrowing them lessens significantly the danger of a psychotic regression.

Resistance is seen as a counterforce that is activated at the beginning of treatment, when the patient is directed to talk. "As this counterforce waxes and wanes, it gives rise to countless manifestations which the analyst recognizes and deals with as *resistance*. Attempts to overcome the resistance of an extremely narcissistic patient serve to intensify the counterforce. In order to diminish it, the pressure for progress is carefully controlled" (p. 144). The patient's patterns of resistance are also viewed as holding operations that the patient resorts to to maintain his psychological equilibrium in other life situations, as well as in treatment. Accordingly, their survival function is recognized and respected.

Additionally, resistance is seen as performing a communication function by conveying the behaviors that the patient had to utilize in preserving his ego in his crucial early years.

The modifications of the standard approach to resistance were organized by Spotnitz (1969b) in an approach he termed "modern psychoanalysis." In his book, Spotnitz notes the standard procedures for dealing with resistance: confrontation, clarification, interpretation, and working-through, with primary reliance on interpretation and the attendant achievement of insight by the patient. He describes his method as a distillation of the classical approach that is in evidence from the opening of the case when "the therapist demonstrates the attitude that the patient has the right to resist" (p. 111).

CHAPTER 2

The Concept of Resistance in Group Psychotherapy

Before we review the develop-
ment of the concept of resistance in group therapy, an outline
of the history of the group-treatment approach is appropriate.

The pioneer period of group therapy is generally considered
to extend from 1907 to the early 1930s, and those most
frequently associated with this period include Pratt, Lazell,
Marsh, Burrow, Adler, and Moreno.

In 1905, Dr. Joseph Pratt, a Boston internist, organized the
"home sanitorium" treatment of consumption at the outpatient
clinic of Massachusetts General Hospital. His weekly meeting
with indigent patients was admittedly a timesaving device; his
brief inspirational talks were given to help patients maintain
the hygienic regimen he prescribed. Pratt's awareness of some
of the psychological dividends of group membership—feelings
of belonging, mutual support, and identification with fellow
members—is reflected in his description of the weekly meeting
(Pratt 1907): "The Class Meeting is a pleasant social hour for the
members. One confided that the meeting was her weekly
picnic. Made up as our membership is of different races and

sects, they have a common bond in a common disease and a fine spirit of comradery has been developed" (p. 14).

Psychiatrists in mental hospitals were stimulated by the possibilities of Pratt's approach. About 1910, Lazell and Marsh began to apply group methods to the treatment of psychiatric patients, hoping to positively influence poor morale and counteract their isolation and emotional withdrawal. In 1918 Lazell gave a series of lectures to groups of schizophrenic war veterans. He spoke to them in simple language about their war experiences and the causes and symptoms of their illness.

In a 1921 article, Lazell listed the advantages of the group method:

1. The patient's fear of death and of his sexual problems were universalized, with resultant alleviation of feelings of damage and stigma.
2. The patient's fear of the analyst was diminished in the presence of the group.
3. The patient who seemed totally inaccessible was found to have heard and retained much of the lecture.
4. The patient developed positive transference to the speaker and sought individual contact with him.
5. The patient was emotionally activated.

Lazell also noted another distinct advantage of the group method: The patient's problems were reactivated thus unsettling his passive adjustment to the security of the institution.

Marsh, a minister and morale officer in World War I before entering the field of psychiatry, employed techniques he described as the "psychological equivalents of the revival." Working with patient groups that averaged fewer than twenty people, Marsh sought to emotionally stimulate his patients through lectures, discussions, singing, and dancing. The development of a group bond through crowd psychology, morale boosting, and salesmanship made it easier, he stated, to "sell sanity" to members of a group than to a solitary patient in his office. He experimented with the idea of a therapeutic community in which all the personnel would be involved in a common effort to fully develop themselves. He organized lecture series for social workers, occupational therapists, chaplains, medical and nursing personnel, and ward attendants, which focused on helping them to attain self-understanding as a prerequisite to understanding their patients. Each participant was asked to make a personality chart that traced his own emotional development. At Worcester State Hospital, Marsh utilized the hospital radio equipment to deliver mental-hygiene courses and lectures to the patients. Stressing the social and environmental aspects of mental illness, he adopted the credo: "By the crowd have they been broken; by the crowd shall they be healed" (Marsh 1931, p. 349).

Another pioneering effort was that of Alfred Adler, who, in 1921 in the Vienna School Guidance Clinics, began to counsel children before groups that included social workers, teachers, and physicians studying his procedures. Although Adler's initial purpose was instructional, it was subsequently observed that the group procedure was producing emotional effects among the spectators and favorable effects in the therapist-patient relationship.

Trigant Burrow (1927) is recognized as the first American psychoanalyst to practice group therapy. A pupil of Freud who later developed a social theory of behavior called phyloanalysis, Burrow began his private practice of group analysis in 1918. He and his students analyzed one another in experimental laboratory groups of from four to twenty members. In general, Burrow felt that the Freudian emphasis on the individual and his phenomenology was wrong. Burrow felt there were no individuals in society, only members of groups. Since his group activities were primarily oriented to social research, rather than to therapy, and because he gave up his groups to devote himself to the development of his social theories, Burrow did not heavily influence events in group therapy.

Moreno is considered to have played a role in propagating the more recent phase of group therapy. His name is most identified with the application of role-playing in the framework of group psychotherapy and psychodrama, an approach he developed in experiments with groups in Vienna before World

War I. (While a medical student, he attempted to help prostitutes rehabilitate themselves through group procedures.) In 1932, Moreno introduced the term *group therapy* to describe a method of grouping prisoners so their interactions would be mutually beneficial.

Louis Wender is considered to be one of the first to conduct psychoanalytically oriented groups, having done so in a hospital setting in 1930. Like Pratt, Lazell, and Marsh before him, Wender (1936) utilized lectures and theoretical discussion. He described his approach as being based on the following assumption:

> The application of some of the hypotheses and methods of psychoanalysis, when applied to a group for the purposes of treatment, will lead to the release of certain emotional conflicts and a partial reorganization of the personality and ultimately to an increased capacity for social amalgamation. [p. 54]

Wender's group sessions were begun with lectures on instinctual drives, conscious and unconscious elements of the mind, the significance of dreams, early infantile traumatism, and the varying defense mechanisms. Wender reported that "a sense of intimacy within the group develops, greater freedom from inhibition is observed in theoretical discussions and is followed by a spontaneous readiness on the part of some patients to discuss their own problems" (p. 55). Along with insight, patient-to-patient transference, and reality checking through group interaction, Wender listed "catharsis-in-the-family" as a basic dynamic of his group approach (referring to the patient experiencing a significant degree of acceptance, respect, and love within a symbolic family setting provided by the group).

Paul Schilder, a prominent psychiatrist, began work with therapeutic groups in 1935 at Bellevue Hospital in New York. Each patient was seen individually before joining the group, and individual sessions continued in conjunction with group sessions. Schilder also began group sessions in a structured way, with studies of case histories of group members. These histories were based on an elaborate set of questions that elicited information about the patient's life history, including early infantile material, fantasies, familial relationships, and sexual development. After review and study of a member's case history, a freer type of discussion ensued, which Schilder described as a form of free association. Dream interpretation was also a standard feature of Schilder's group treatment. He specifically advocated the use of group therapy in alleviating the patient's feelings of being isolated. He reported that a group member's recall of sexual feelings toward his sister evoked similar memories in other members, and stated: "The relief patients experience when they no longer feel excluded from the community because of their urges and desires that society does not openly tolerate is remarkable" (p. 90).

Schilder noted that many of the cases treated in the groups could not have achieved as good results in individual analysis. He suggested group psychotherapy in cases of "social neuroses" characterized by marked discomfort in the presence of others, a reluctance to be observed, and accompanying physical symptoms such as abdominal discomfort, excessive sweating, and blushing.

In 1934, Slavson began applying the concepts of individual psychoanalysis to children's groups at the Jewish Board of Guardians in New York. He developed activity group therapy, a group-treatment modality widely used today with children in the 8–12 age range. This approach (1943) utilizes a highly permissive setting in which the children express and discharge their pent-up feelings in the presence of an unconditionally loving therapist. In this method Slavson stressed the corrective impact of the dynamics of regression, the positive transference toward and identification with the therapist, the cathartic expression of feelings of anger toward sibling figures in the group, and the strengthening of the self-image through acceptance by the group "family." As he extended his work to adolescents and adults, Slavson (1950) termed his approach "analytic group psychotherapy," which he defined as directly descended from psychoanalysis:

Analytic group psychotherapy employs transference, catharsis, interpretation of latent content of the patients'
communication; it deals with infantile sexuality, the unconscious, the basic hostility of man's nature and accepts
the inherent intrapsychic conflict between the id and
superego and its effect in determining of character, personality and pathology. [p. 18]

Alexander Wolf, a New York psychoanalyst, began working
with groups in his private practice in 1938. He described his
work as "psychoanalysis in groups," based on the four pillars
of Freudian psychoanalysis: dream interpretation, free association, the analysis of transference, and resistance. He assumed
that the patient's repressed memories were as accessible in a
group situation as in individual psychoanalysis, and that they
were explorable through the techniques of free association and
dream analysis.

The slow but steady development of group therapy in
institutional and community settings was tremendously cat-
alyzed by World War II, when military psychiatrists were faced
with huge caseloads. Psychotherapists improvised, tested, and
developed a wide array of group approaches to deal with the
streams of patients suffering from battle fatigue, acute anxiety
states, hysteria, and other disturbances. On returning to civil-
ian life, many therapists who had worked with groups in a
military setting began to use group therapy in their private
practices or became affiliated with similar treatment programs
in hospitals and social agencies. Extensive research in group
treatment, conducted by Powdermaker and Frank in Veterans'
Administration hospitals, stimulated the awareness and
growth of group therapy in this country.

POST-WAR CONTRIBUTIONS

The first published contribution dealing specifically with resistance in group therapy was made by Fritz Redl. In his paper,
Redl offered observations on resistances demonstrated by

individual members of groups of delinquent adolescents. He indicated there are "group psychological defenses against change and treatment reaching far beyond the scope of individual behavior" (Redl 1948, p. 307). He identified several of these group resistances, including "escape into love," whereby the group lures the therapist into a loving relationship while maintaining their delinquent behavior outside the group. Also cited was "protective provocation," whereby the group courts rejection by the therapist to avoid treatment and growing up.

In his comprehensive paper "The Psychoanalysis of Groups" Wolf (1949–1950) saw the analysis of resistance as one of the basic stages in his method. Wolf observed that the group setting provides a special environment lending itself to the elaboration of resistive forms peculiar to it, and he identified some of the most commonly encountered ones. "Fickle transference love," where a patient claims to be in love with the analyst but soon becomes emotionally attached to another group member, is confronted in the group as a compulsive pattern. Another manifestation of resistance is the "compulsive missionary spirit who persists in looking after group members in a supportive parental way, using this device to subtly dominate and to repress more basic feelings. The group always resents this false charity and demands and evokes more spontaneous participation from the messianic" (Wolf 1949–1950, p. 38). Voyeurism, a resistance unique to the group setting, is utilized by those patients

who try to escape personal examination and engagement by taking grandstand seats which give them a gratifying view of what may be the equivalent of the primal scene. They seem willing and even eager to allow others full interaction, while they assign to themselves a tremulous watchfulness. [p. 39]

Hiding behind the analysis of others is portrayed as a common resistance in a group situation, which provides a convenient setting for its exercise. This is characterized by a concentration on the neurotic behavior of other patients, with an accompanying evasion of analysis directed toward oneself. The use of history as resistance is seen in patients who produce long, irrelevant biographies as a form of evasion. Reluctance to discuss sexuality is also listed.

Wolf notes that resistances are as manifold and distinct as human beings themselves. Some try to hide in the group; some seek to escape into a group from individual treatment. Some exhibit contempt and a supercilious avoidance of members they regard as inferior. Some seek to overwhelm the group "with endless outpourings of irrelevant talk" (Wolf 1949–1950, p. 43).

Wolf also observed that the catalytic atmosphere of mutual revelation in the group setting exerted a significant influence in dissolving resistance.

Wolf and colleagues (1954) later addressed the resistance of sexual acting out among group members. Although they recognized its resistive and destructive aspects, they suggested such behavior had constructive potential for the working through of conflicts.

From 1948 to 1951, W. R. Bion, a British psychiatrist, wrote a series of influential articles in which he postulated concepts of unconscious basic assumptions underlying the behavior of groups. Every group was seen as having two aspects, or two different modes of behavior: the "work group" and the "basic-assumption group." The work group is that aspect of group functioning that has to do with the real, stated task of the group and therefore attempts to be organized, rational, purposeful, and constructive. Beneath this overt, conscious level, Bion sees the life of the group as entirely different. On this latent level, group members come and stay together because of strong needs that are embodied in their basic assumptions. Bion (1948–1951) suggested that these emotional forces fall into three distinct categories: dependency, fight-flight, and pairing.

The essential aim of the basic-assumption dependency group is to attain security through the leader. Members act in an inadequate and immature manner, as if to imply that the leader, by contrast, is omnipotent. Benefit is not felt to come from other members, but from the leader alone, with the result that members feel they are being treated only when talking to the leader. The leader is thus idealized and made into a godlike parent who will care for his little children.

The second assumption is that the group has met to preserve itself and this can only be done by fighting (someone or something) or fleeing. Such a group is, in Bion's view, dominated by the need for action, and tends to be anti-intellectual and opposed to the idea of self-examination. The leader is expected to mobilize the group for attack or lead it in flight.

In pairing, the assumption is that the group has met for purposes of reproduction and to bring forth someone who will act as a savior. To achieve this end, two members are selected to symbolically "get together" and carry out the pairing task; thus, the group may tolerate and encourage a strong emotional tie between two of its members. A group dominated by this assumption is pervaded by an atmosphere of eager hopefulness and optimism. The group climate is one of pleasant agreeableness beneath which, Bion suggests, is considerable aggression.

These basic assumptions represent obstacles to the fulfillment of the group's stated goals and can be seen as major sources of resistance in the group setting. The basic-assumption phenomena appear to be conceptualizations of similar forces discussed by Spotnitz in his formulations of the inadequacy (dependency), reproductive (pairing), and negative-reproductive (fight–flight) constellations.

Spotnitz and Gabriel (1950) described how emotional currents operate as resistances to the therapeutic process. One type, the "reproductive constellation," comprised those forces in adolescent girls and mothers that are present in the desire for sexual gratification, pregnancy, and the wish for a healthy child. The "inadequacy constellation" concerned the emotional and physical inadequacies that deterred individuals from fulfilling the goals of the reproductive constellation. These inadequacies were evidenced in pervasive feelings of inadequacy, inability to cope with the demands of school and work, and feelings that legitimate sexual satisfaction was unattainable.

In resistances based on the inadequacy constellation, the

groups reacted with inadequacy when confronted with the therapist's request that they tell their life stories. The reproductive constellation operated as resistance when group members sought gratification by talking about sex and seeking immediate satisfaction for genital and related pleasures, rather than trying to understand themselves and one another. As Redl had done, the authors identified resistances of individuals and of the group as a whole.

A third category of resistances, one induced in the therapist by the group, was also identified. The idea was introduced that group members tend to deal with one another's individual resistances "so that eventually they could unite in dealing with the therapist who was not gratifying them" (Spotnitz and Gabriel 1950, p. 77). It was noted that the resistances served a significant function: Their maintenance helped the members "to adjust to the forces stimulated by the immediate stresses due to the operation of the inadequacy and reproductive constellation. The utilization of resistances served to preserve the status quo and to maintain the existing relationships" (p. 84).

Spotnitz's next paper (1952a) represented a seminal contribution on several levels. First, it clarified the nature of resistance in the group setting. Second, it brought the new field of group psychotherapy under the umbrella of long-established Freudian concepts, while simultaneously explaining some of the basic dynamics of resistance as molded by the group setting. The same types of resistances delineated by Freud in individual analysis also appear in the course of group therapy. Spotnitz suggested that the individual resistances of group members may unite to become a group resistance, which is defined as the same form of resistance being used by all or a majority of group members at the same time. In this paper, Spotnitz offered an understanding of resistance as an effort—on the part of an individual or a group—to hold a feeling in check. It was also suggested that the resistance could not be effectively dealt with until the emotional forces behind it were understood.

In another contribution, Spotnitz (1952b) offered the following definition of resistance: "When individuals are gathered in a group for therapeutic purposes and are directed to give an account of their life histories, feelings, and thoughts in a spontaneous, emotional, significant way, it is natural that they will find it difficult to do so, and the voluntary and involuntary methods they use to avoid presenting the desired material are considered the resistances" (p. 95). He also observed that the resistances of the individual patient are strengthened in a group setting through the presence of diverse personalities. The need for increased use of regression as a defense is therefore significantly lessened. Instead, less dangerous defenses are adequate for the individual, and the therapist can study these at a more leisurely pace, with less danger to the emotional stability of the individual patient. The main task of the therapist is defined as "how to deal with the resistances that are common to all members of the group in their relationship to him" (p. 92).

Spotnitz presented two fundamental differences in the operation and handling of resistance in group and individual therapy. First, group members tend to deal with one another's resistances. This may be done constructively or destructively, and it is the therapist's task to enlist cooperation among group members in dealing constructively with one another's resistances. Second, group members tend to develop a common (group) resistance.

Spotnitz also applied Glover's concept of counterresistance to the position of the group therapist: "The common resistances of the group tend to stimulate in the group therapist counter-resistances" (p. 85).

FURTHER CONTRIBUTIONS: 1950–1955

In the early 1950s, other clinicians began to identify varied resistances in the group setting.

Prados (1951) found that the adjunctive use of films was effective in overcoming resistance in group therapy, especially in loosening the barriers of repression. He emphasized the value of group therapy in helping patients achieve insight into their defense mechanisms. The dynamic processes in the group setting broke down narcissistic barriers, thus rendering it easier to deal with many resistances that would be difficult to recognize and handle in individual therapy.

Prados (1953) also focused on the reactions of patients in individual therapy to the invitation to join a group as a fruitful opportunity for the uncovering of a series of resistances that extended into the patient's early group sessions. He observed that the feeling of being supported by the group makes the patient more capable of withstanding his impulses. This reduces the danger of regression more than individual therapy.

A group of clinicians at Johns Hopkins Hospital (Frank et al. 1952), identified several consistent behavioral patterns of resistance that they observed in early sessions of therapy groups. These behavioral types are termed the "help-rejecting complainer" and the "doctor's assistant." The first continually clamors for attention to his problem and simultaneously rejects any advice offered, maintaining the helplessness of his situation. The second pattern reveals itself in a patronizing, help-offering attitude toward other patients: the giving of repressive, trite advice and the stimulation of others to express their difficulties. When pressed to reveal themselves, these "assistants" tend to withdraw from treatment.

In a subsequent paper from this group, Rosenthal and colleagues (1954) described the "self-righteous moralist," whose major characterological pattern is the need to be right and to prove others wrong, particularly in regard to moral issues such as justice, sacrifice, responsibility, and gratitude. Such an individual manages to become the central figure by indefinitely reiterating his position. He shows no ability to concede, compromise, or admit error, and demonstrates no awareness of his effect upon other group members. In the area of therapeutic management, the authors emphasize that this type of patient needs early support for his need for status, while other members may simultaneously need protection from him.

In a discussion of transference in group therapy, Glatzer

(1952) noted that the presence of others admitting to difficulties has a significant loosening effect on previously suspicious and highly resistive patients. The inclusion of diverse personalities in groups is recommended as productive of intragroup transference and the erosion of resistance.

Glatzer (1953) also observed that positive transference seems to be facilitated by the group, which is helpful in overcoming initial resistances. However, she cautioned alertness to the resistances of negative feelings underlying the positive transference, and deemed it an error for therapists to encourage the prolongation of the positive aspect. She warned that "unless individual resistance is penetrated, there is danger it may spill over and turn the whole group against the therapist" (p. 41).

A focus on transference resistances was presented by Taylor (1952). Resistances discussed included patients displacing aggression against one another, scapegoating, leakage from group discussions, silence, formation of conspiratorial friendships outside the group, and turning of group discussion into mere symptom description. One form of transference resistance, erotic contact outside the group, was effectively handled by the issuance of "prophylactic predictions" (p. 133) of such behavior by the therapist. It was noted that certain patients—who occupy dominant positions in the group but are unpopular—show high incidence of premature termination. This resistance of the "flight of the deputy leader" is handled by predicting his withdrawal and initiating discussion of the feelings he induces in the group.

In their comprehensive research project on group therapy in Veterans' Administration hospital settings, Powdermaker and Frank (1953) pointed to resistance of the whole group as "one of the greatest challenges to the therapist's skill" (p. 384). They accepted the necessity of dealing with it and suggested some techniques. They also reported that the resolution of resistance in a patient was often facilitated by other group members. A resistant member might begin to participate as the protégé of another patient with whom he identifies. He may follow the leader of another patient who expressed feelings similar to his own and was accepted by the group. The group itself may convince the reluctant patient that his underlying feelings are more acceptable than his defense.

Shea (1954) compared resistance reactions in individual and group psychotherapy, noting that: (1) group therapy makes possible for some patients the dissolution of resistances that are intractable in individual therapy; and (2) in still other patients, whose resistances would eventually succumb to individual treatment, the group setting markedly catalyzes the process.

Durkin (1954), in a book on the group therapy of mothers, saw the nature and management of resistance in group therapy basically the same as in individual therapy. However, she noted some special conditions of group therapy affecting resistance. These refer to group members sometimes reinforcing one another's resistances, sometimes helping to fight them. Additionally, certain resistances are easily hidden in the group setting. For example, the patient with strong voyeuristic tendencies who appears eager to help another member by questioning her about her feelings and various aspects of her life. The exhibitionistic patient may enact her unconscious impulse through the giving of seemingly valuable material of a sexual nature. The defense of living by proxy may also be concealed within the group fabric. In the same way, in sexually homogenous groups, homosexual feelings can be unconsciously gratified by talking about otherwise forbidden subjects. Intense transference feelings among members may be acted out between sessions and lead to withdrawal from group participation, a situation to be forestalled, the author indicates, by early interpretation of growing transferences.

Durkin observed that patients with similar defenses tend to have blind spots for one another's resistances. Durkin gave special attention to character resistance, noting that groups act as a magnifying glass for the examination of character. Members connect on one another's ingrained attitudes and patterns: "You're always so dignified," or "You always have that smile." The unified weight of group opinion can exert a powerful impact on even rigid character traits.

In their remarks on the special features of group therapy and their implications for the selection of patients, Freedman and

Sweet (1954) noted a special aspect of resistance they termed "sibling support." In this situation, some or all of the members cooperate with a defensive member in warding off a threat of therapeutic participation. Such concerted group activity serves to support individual resistance by obscuring its true significance as resistance. The group setting is seen as offering opportunities for the freer play of resistances, permitting patients to refrain from participation and emotional involvement, which allows more prolonged periods of resistance than individual treatment. The presence of other forces in the group that work to dissolve resistance, such as the mutual stimulation of members, is acknowledged.

Fried (1955) described the therapeutic benefit of combined individual and group therapy for passive-narcissistic patients. The monotonously friendly, seemingly cooperative, submissive behavior demonstrated by these patients in individual therapy is seen as evidence of "the intense resistance to any reorganization of the personality." This resistance and the resistive barrier of narcissism are breached in the group setting, where such patients are enabled to experience their hostility.

Mann (1955) presented the thesis of a powerful group-destructive resistance: "Any group tends to mobilize very quickly its disruptive forces in an attempt to provoke dissolution of the group so as to avoid tender, constructive, self-sacrificing libidinal investments in the therapist and in each other. The chief weapon in the service of the need is hostility" (p. 237). Fear of terrible retaliation for sexual and aggressive fantasies is viewed as giving rise to the "enormous resistances against the kind of close participation that is offered to the members" (p. 237).

Morse and colleagues (1955) presented a case illustration of the effect of group therapy in diminishing resistance to individual treatment. The patient, highly guarded and suspicious, adhered rigidly to the stand that he had been perfectly well until his military service and any discussions of childhood events and familial relations were therefore irrelevant. Any attempt to guide therapeutic discussion in those directions during individual therapy was met with strong resistance. In the group setting, the patient was exposed to peers who revealed the early childhood bases for their current illnesses. The patient soon became more productive and spontaneous in individual therapy; his identification with other group members was seen as the chief tool in the resolution of his resistance.

The resistances of orally dependent patients in group therapy were examined by Beukenkamp (1955). Such patients seek an exclusive relationship with the therapist and enter the group with no investment in any of its members. When the therapist does not respond to their demands for dependency, the resultant frustration can activate oral-sadistic behavior. Some sit defiantly on the periphery of the group; others ask repeatedly, "What are we to do here?" and "What is expected of me?" Some take it upon themselves to be the "teachers" or "junior therapists" as a denial of their own wishes to be cared for and fed. Dissolution of these resistances is accomplished through the group becoming the "protective parent" and by the therapist gratifying the oral hunger by paraphrasing what these patients have said, rather than by interpreting the material.

Cameron and Stewart (1955) reported on resistances encountered in group therapy with chronically neurotic patients in a hospital setting. One such resistance, termed "failure of theme development," involved casual social conversation about unconnected subjects, which ultimately took the form of silence that was a chronic group resistance. Acting out, irregular attendance, and intense hostility to new members (which effectively closed the group to new patients) were also resistances in evidence.

CONTRIBUTIONS: 1956–1959

In 1956, Cameron and Freeman discussed the resistances they encountered in group therapy with inpatients suffering from depressive reactions. Resistances were classified as either belonging to the group as a whole or to individuals. Group resistances were expressed in silences, in permitting one member to deliver prolonged monologues, or by a majority of the group engaging one member in discussion of innocuous material. Quarreling by subgroups was reported as another expression of group resistance. Withholding of information, deflection, absenteeism, and avoidance of discussion of one's own sexuality were mentioned as individual resistances. In dealing with the resistances, the writers utilized interpretation addressed and limited to the immediate group situation and in the context of the group as a whole. The interpretation of negative transference allusions, in which the group would discuss how various doctors had erred in treating them, resulted in their becoming aware of this latent hostility against the therapists. After awhile, the patients learned to anticipate these negative-transference interpretations, and this was employed as a group resistance. The therapist observed that groupwide interpretations were then not personal enough to allow the patients to react to them emotionally; subsequently, individual interpretations of resistance and transference were made.

In their description of an adolescent group-therapy program, Becker and colleagues (1956) paid special attention to the individual member's resistances. Among those reported were the expansive, narcissistic youth who overwhelms the group with his charm; the critical attitudes of the perfectionistic youngster who may withdraw into silence or scornful aloofness; the self-effacing and ingratiating youth; and the resigned member who needs constant encouragement to participate.

Bross (1966) evaluated some of the factors involved in premature termination of patients in group therapy. The dynamics reported included: feelings of rejection by the group "family"; strong dependency needs that promote repetitious testing of the therapist and group; intense anxiety generated by group interactions; fear of the unknown—"a frightening awareness of disorganized and destructive unconscious impulses which force abandoning the group to forestall a breakdown of ego defenses" (p. 392).

Slavson (1956) examined the nature and treatment of acting-out resistance in group therapy and noted that the ego finds, in acting out, "a shorter, easier and more primitively direct route to discharge anxiety, guilt and aggression than working it through by the prolonged and arduous road to verbalization and insight" (p. 11). *Acting out* is defined as the "transmutation of emotional tension into physical expression that may stem from temperamental dispositions or psychogenic stress and from inadequate ego controls of general or specific inpulses" (p. 9). The author describes a variety of acting-out resistances. Acting out through aggression, withdrawal, or silence may appear: as a reaction to fear and anxiety in the group situation; as provocation based on masochistic need or latent homosexuality; as striving for status through exhibitionism, domination, and rivalry; as "emotional hypochondriasis" based on the yearning to be pitied and to receive sympathy. Slavson observes that acting out can be contagious and thus become a group phenomenon of resistance. The acting-out syndrome of compulsive talking is focused on as a resistance that has a very adverse effect on groups. The transference nature of acting out is stressed.

Durkin (1956) reviewed group psychotherapy with mothers and presented two forms of resistance to which mothers' groups are especially prone. First, after the initial phase of the group, they revert to talking about children, usually as a defense against repressed aggression or sexuality that is displaced onto the child. Second, they talk of sexual material, which seems valuable, but is essentially a disguised enactment of their homosexual feelings toward one another or the female therapist.

In a review of group therapy with patients suffering from psychosomatic disorders, Stein (1956) recognized in these patients a powerful resistance to the idea that their somatic complaints had psychogenic causes. This resistance strongly united the group in aggressive attitudes toward the therapist.

In an evaluation of the dynamic factors involved in the treatment of borderline schizophrenics in group therapy, Spotnitz (1957b) noted that resistances are not *overcome*, but *outgrown*. The resistances exhibited by this type of patient are identified as resistance to spontaneous emotional communication, a disinclination to function democratically in the group, and a strong reluctance to release hostile or loving feelings in language.

The group dynamics of acting-out resistance were articulated by Ziferstein and Grotjahn (1957): (1) Acting out is more common in group therapy, because tendencies to act out are stimulated by the unconscious impulses and anxieties of other members. (2) Acting out is therapeutically useful only as a transition to understanding. Essentially it is a resistance—at times a dangerous one—and it should be treated as such. (3) Interpretation, consistently applied, results in the recovery of the memories and associations that are being enacted rather than remembered.

In studying the emergence of common forms of resistance in group therapy, Kotkov (1957a) presented the categories of control and avoidance of feeling, denial of emotion and anxiety, and belligerence and antagonism. These reactions that permeate resistance are manifested through difficulties in speaking, antagonistic reactions, mobilization of symptoms, and queries about the efficacy of treatment.

Kotkov discusses silence as a protection against the discovery of weakness, a defense against revelation of hostile fantasies, a defense against punishment and rejection, and as an expression of ambivalence toward treatment. Antagonistic reactions are viewed as a hostile defense against treatment and the emotional acceptance of illness. They are also seen as: a reaction to fear; displacement from traumatic experiences of the past; a defense against guilt from gratification (i.e., the acceptance and attention they receive from the group, to which they feel unentitled); and defense against developing positive feelings toward others in the group. In the category of mobilization of symptoms, the author cites obstinate attempts to blame psychological symptoms on physical causes: "They have a desperate desire to retreat into the organic in order to escape talking about their thoughts. They flee into their symptoms when threatened by situations which recall infantile fears of inadequacy" (Kotkov 1957a, p. 94). Obsessions, the author states, "are used as an escape from subjectively exaggerated responsibility and the conviction of failure with attendant anxiety" (p. 95). The author suggests that group therapy should centralize its efforts on resistances, rather than place pressure on the recollection of experiences. "The clearance of resistance promotes the birth of insight" (p. 88). It is also noted that "resistances of the individual become mobilized as resistances of the group" (p. 88).

In another paper, Kotkov (1957b) examined the resistance to discussing sex in group therapy and emphasized that members need encouragement to face their sexual thoughts. He presented frequently encountered sexual fantasies and anxieties.

In remarks on group therapy with antisocial adolescents, Schulman (1957) stated that the resistance encountered is basically the delinquent's character resistance to conformity and cooperative behavior. It is noted that interpretation of group silence seems to create added anxiety that could lead to physical acting out.

The resistances of institutionalized delinquents in group therapy were enumerated by Shellow and colleagues (1958). The initial resistances against relating are manifested by irrelevant gossip that serves as a smoke screen between the group and the therapist. The verbally facile members lead the flight into trivia, while others reveal their anxiety by sleeping or answering the therapist's direct questions with noncommittal, monosyllabic responses. The role of the con man—the skillful manipulator of others—in leading this resistance is recognized. The next stage of resistance takes the form of the projection of the group's defensive hostility toward the therapist into the surrounding institutional life. A following resistance involves making demands upon the therapist, in order to validate their belief that he is just another hateful, depriving adult. A final group resistance, apparently similar to Redl's "protective provocation," is a direct attack upon the therapist, to keep him at a distance.

Bowers and co-authors (1958) discussed the resistances presented by religious personnel in group therapy. Their verbal proficiency, facility for dialectic thinking, and tendencies to monopolize could be used in the service of powerful resistances to cooperative group functioning. A destructive resistance manifested was the expression of severe condemnatory attitudes employed to drive weaker members out of the group. The management of these resistances was based on the emotional reactions of other group members, "in having sufficient people in the group who are not impressed, who demand that the language of the group be nonprofessional, who become quite angry when 'churchy' language is used, who are quite capable of fighting back when attacked" (p. 247).

Jackson and Grotjahn (1958) evaluated the treatment of an oral dependent and demanding character neurosis in a woman patient in individual and group-therapy settings. Individual settings offered excessive oral gratification to the patient. "She accepted interpretations like mother's milk by incorporating them like mother's milk and not by integrating them at a mature level of functioning" (p. 375). Her main resistance in the group was a refusal to participate, being unwilling to emotionally join the group and share the therapist as a mother. She remained in the group only because of the positive transference to her therapist in individual therapy. When the group pointed out her nonparticipation, she parried by replying that since she had individual sessions and other members did not, she would feel guilty taking the group's time for herself. Under constant group pressure, she would participate, but only in a reversal of roles, where she would feed advice and interpretation to other dependent members. Threats to leave the group were also employed. The shift of her transference neurosis from the individual to the group setting removed the therapist as the exclusive focus of her neurosis and permitted the group to effectively intervene; this led to the emergence into consciousness of her oral need for sole possession of the therapist.

Moses and Schwartz (1958) explain the defense mechanisms utilized by prisoners to allay the anxiety aroused in them by group therapy. The most frequently used mechanism was the "party line" that presents the inmate as having been perpetually "bum-rapped." In this view, the administration is pictured as exclusively concerned with keeping prisons filled to capacity

and with holding prisoners longer than is reasonable or necessary. The prisoner, in this view, is characterized as reasonable,
wronged, and responsible. When the "party line" defense
failed, group members employed the resistance of seeking to
force the therapists "to declare themselves either as the repre-
sentatives of an angry, primitive, rejecting society, or as the
messianic emissaries of the bum-rapped, maltreated and misunderstood inmate population in their crusade for justice"
(p. 455).

In a far-ranging review of the field of group therapy, Slavson
(1959) described the essential dynamics of the various forms of
group therapy according to the types of transference, catharsis,
insight, reality testing, sublimation, and resistance that
emerged. Individual resistances listed as appearing in analytic
group therapy are: displacement, deflection, distraction,
planned communication, irrelevancy, silence, absence, lateness, and acting out.

CONTRIBUTIONS: 1959–1980

In his book *The Couch and the Circle*, Spotnitz (1961b) presented
his approach to resistance in the group setting. He recognizes
that patients are incapable of consistently engaging in the kind
of verbal communication demanded of them at the beginning
of treatment. Patients frequently need to resist talking about
themselves in order to monitor their emotional balance in the
group. Accordingly, Spotnitz often supports members' needs
to resist talking, so he can study the origins and purpose of the
resistance.

Goodman and colleagues (1964) offer cross sections of therapist–group interaction in which the therapist enhanced or
induced group resistance. The authors posit: "The phenomenon of a therapy group in a state of resistance, which the
therapist recognizes but is unable to deal with, is likely to be
related integrally to a counter-transference distortion of the
therapist" (p. 343). They suggest that many premature termi-
nations of treatment are based on the therapist's inability,

because of his own conflicts, to act constructively in the face of resistance.

Mally and Ogston (1964) summarized a group-therapy experience with patients with chronic physical complaints and functional symptoms. A primary resistance they displayed was competition for the position of being the "sickest," in hopes of winning the sole concern of the co-leaders. On the other hand, they supported one another's resistances to understanding themselves and the maintaining of their status as being ill. Their life histories were recounted to obtain pity rather than understanding.

Ormont (1964) described the resolution of tenacious individual resistances through a combination of individual and group therapy settings employing two analysts, plus an optional setting of group sessions without the group analyst. The therapeutically useful parameters observed are presented as:

1. Multiple transferences: The patient's intense transference in the individual setting is dealt with by establishing, via the group, other, less intense transferences in which he is more accessible.
2. Multiple interpreters: The group setting adds "multiple interpreters who validate the patient's attitudes and actions."
3. Multiple countertransference reactions: The patient is better understood, and his reactions better dealt with, as both therapists use and compare their induced feelings.
4. Multiple settings: The patient's selective functioning in the different settings is utilized in working through special resistances.

Ormont continued his interest in the study of resistance phenomena and the identification of groupwide manifestations of resistance. In the first of a series of papers, Ormont (1968) defined group resistance as "a collective reluctance to fulfill the terms of the therapeutic contract. Such a resistance is at work whenever the group ignores, overlooks, encourages, or tolerates a violation of the analytic contract by one or more of its members" (p. 147). Illustrations of groupwide resistance and its management are presented.

In his next paper, Ormont (1969) discussed "acting in resistances wherein instead of relating the emotionally significant story of his life in words, the patient may communicate it in action, dramatizing the story through his behavior in the group" (p. 420). Verbal and physical acting out are differentiated.

Ormont (1970–1971) developed Spotnitz's notion that the feelings induced in the therapist by his patients could be developed into a defined instrument for resolving patients' resistances:

Like the individual analyst, the group analyst, if he is in empathic resonance with the group's emotional vibrations, will experience powerful feelings as a natural product of the total group interaction. They are vital, if primitive messages he is receiving from the members' shared unconscious emotions. [p. 96]

Next Ormont (1974) presented techniques involving emotional, symbolic, and joining interventions for the resolution of resistances originating in the preoedipal period of emotional development.

Slavson (1964) elucidated the dynamics of the frequently encountered resistance of silence in group therapy and discerned four types: general and selective individual silences and general and selective silences of the group. Selective individual silence, when it contains negative attitudes of anger, spite, and resentment, is seen as caused by a variety of dynamic factors that may at times signify a "resistive phalanx to the ongoing therapeutic process mobilized by predominant negative transference toward the therapist or prevalent general hostility on the part of group members at a given time" (p. 398). Slavson also notes that group silence may often represent reflection upon a significant group event or feeling. Interpretation of the transference is recommended in the face of resistive phalanx silence.

Aronson (1967) offered criteria for resistance in individual and group therapy. He defined individual resistance as "any diminution in the efficiency of the patient's task behavior during therapy sessions" (p. 87). The author suggests that the most difficult technical problem confronting the group therapist is the recognition and resolution of the simultaneous resistances of most or all of the patients. This group resistance is defined as "a decrease in the operating efficiency of a therapy group manifested by a heightening of the transferential projections, defenses and defensive maneuvers of most or all patients and a joining together of their individual resistances into a common resistive pattern" (p. 94).

Aronson attributes the presence of group resistance to therapeutic error, in that it "presupposes that the therapist has failed to deal adequately with the individual resistances of group patients in his prior contact with them in individual therapy or in the group" (Aronson 1967, p. 92). Among such errors, the author mentions premature placement of patients into group therapy, delay in intervening to analyze and work through individual resistances, and, most crucial, failure to analyze and work through the reactions of group members to some common stimulus impinging strongly on all or most of them. In this last category of factors, countertransference attitudes and actions are the most likely contributors.

Two contributions by Spotnitz embrace his formulations, techniques, and general approach to resistance in the group setting. In a 1968 paper, Spotnitz charted a sequence of resistance patterns that shows the urgency of recognizing and intervening in these "characteristic modes of uncooperative behavior" (p. 16). First priority is accorded to treatment-destructive resistance—"any type of behavior which if permitted to continue would imperil the group's existence or seriously damage any one of its members" (p. 13).

The next stage, status quo (inertia) resistance, usually appears after the first six months, when the members' presenting problems have been somewhat alleviated. This resistance reflects the group's feeling that maintenance of the present state of functioning is all that can be asked of them. This is demonstrated by their wish to drift along aimlessly and have a good time together. Resistance to analytic progress contains more anxiety than status quo patterns and represents fear of change and apprehension about moving ahead into unknown emotional areas.

Fourth priority is accorded to resistance to teamwork, which involves self-preoccupation, desires for undivided attention, and an unwillingness to listen to or learn from others. A fifth level in this system of priorities is reached in resistance to termination, which features a return to patterns of resistive and uncooperative behavior that had seemingly been outgrown but reappear during the final months of treatment and before the vacation break.

In another paper, Spotnitz (1969a) gave an overview of resistance phenomena in group therapy. Freud's concept of resistance and his categorization of it are reviewed and placed into the perspective of the group setting. The suggestion is made that the group be involved in a concurrence of opinion as to what constitutes resistive behavior. The author states that "the total ideal situation for recognizing and analyzing irrational and inappropriate behavior obtains when the group members have consciously accepted it as a resistance pattern" (p. 212).

Gadpaille (1959) studied resistance in groups of delinquent adolescents, and observed that the very existence of the group as a therapeutic milieu permits types of resistance that vary from those seen in individual therapy. The presence of other patients allows for side conversations, mutual support by avoidance, and deflection of feelings. In a reference to group resistance, the author noted that "there is often a contagiousness, a totality of response in which the individuality of the patients is submerged by a total group attitude" (p. 277).

The earliest resistances of these groups were organized against projected external dangers. These organized resistances followed a predictable sequence. First, overt defiance was expressed, verbally and behaviorally, through absence and bodily postures. At times, sizeable numbers would stay away or walk out. The next level of resistance was via testing, to provoke the therapist into retaliatory anger, a pattern also recognized by Redl and Shellow. The threat of group silence was the next level of resistance; but members' needs to defy, complain, and provoke verbally overrode any tendencies of the group as a whole to defend itself with total silence. All of the defenses against projected external dangers were also directed against other members by individuals or subgroups.

Gadpaille concluded that delinquent groups are capable of employing a host of highly organized resistances against external dangers, with great versatility. When the internal conflicts are exposed, a member is prey to anxieties against which he has no prepared defense. "However, the achievement of this stage in therapy is a major step forward" (p. 284).

Leopold (1959) addressed the process of working through conflicts and resistances in group therapy. He saw the availability of multiple channels of communication—patient with therapist, patient with another group member, patient with the group as a whole, and the group with the therapist—as paramount. The patient's constant involvement in and exposure to these levels of interaction enrich and intensify therapy and, when properly utilized, facilitate the process of working through. "They confront the patient with all the bipolar attitudes of his conflict-past and present, fantasy and reality, hate and love" (p. 292).

Mann (1962) gave a theoretical formulation of the group resistance of conformity on different developmental levels. In conformity with what they believe is expected behavior in group therapy, members initially display verbal (oral) aggression toward one another. This is followed by a stage of identification with the leader, in the guise of exceedingly adult behavior that gives a superficial appearance of group cohesion and cooperation. In essence, at this stage passivity is a defense against underlying rebellion. In the next stage, members become occupied with questions of democracy, which represents a maturational advance from the position of conformity. The members engage in a pseudodemocracy, but an underlying sabotage of the group's efforts is in progress. On the next level, the group's hostility toward the leader and their previously disguised rebellious feelings emerge openly. "When the leader's dreaded retaliation fails to materialize, the members realize and express not only their earlier expectations of the group but also begin to recognize the unreality of those expectations" (Mann 1962, p. 10). Following this resolution, resistance is replaced by identification with the constructive aspects of the leader.

In his remarks on the function of the group therapist, Berger (1962) featured dealing with resistance. Citing the analysis of resistance as the hallmark of success in individual and group therapy, he emphasized its centrality. He observed that resistances are chameleonlike in character, capable of assuming new colors and forms in the course of treatment. "Resistance can express itself through action or inaction, silence or works, feeling or non-feeling, overtly or covertly. The resistances of the therapist, individual patients and of the group itself may occur simultaneously, consecutively or intermittently. Each may influence the development of the other" (p. 559).

Group resistances cited by Berger are: silences, absenteeism, lateness, "tea party" discussions of events outside the group, nonpayment of fees by a large segment of the group, decrease in the group's interactional patterns, and withholding of dreams and fantasies.

In his book on the theory, dynamics, and technique of group therapy, Johnson (1963) defined resistance in relationship to the group's working contract: "As soon as the patient begins to react to the stress of the group, he wants to change the contract. Then by drawing attention to the patient's incessant violations of the contract, the therapist can show him how he wants to twist the reality of the contract to suit his own maladaptive patterns" (p. 63). Johnson pays particular attention to silence and acting out as the most troublesome resistances facing the therapist.

In a comprehensive text on group therapy, Slavson (1964) differentiated between those resistances that are common to both individual and group therapy and those that are indigenous to therapy groups. In the former category he listed absenteeism, lateness, deflection, planned communication, irrelevancy, distraction, silence, passivity, and acting out. It was noted that groups afford opportunities for escape from participation that are not available in individual treatment. Slavson also referred to the presence of "inherent solvents of resistance" in groups, such as identification, universalization, and mutual support, which overcome defensive resistances in individuals.

Rosenthal (1968), in a paper on interpretation in group therapy, illustrated the significant impact of members' interpretations to one another in bringing attention to and resolving one another's resistances. The rationale for reflecting back to group members their attitudes and feelings, rather than employing the classical interpretative approach, is clarified and illustrated.

In a series of papers, Rosenthal studied patterns of resistance in a variety of group settings. His paper on adolescent group therapy (1971) clincally illustrated resistances frequently encountered in these groups: craving for excitement, extragroup subgrouping, testing, and denial of inadequacy and damage. The importance of converting negative feeling into language as soon as possible, in order to effectively deter premature termination, was emphasized in a paper (1976) on group-destructive resistance in group therapy. The maturational effect upon a group of the resolution of its major resistances was delineated and illustrated (1979). A sixth paper (1980) depicted the ways in which resistances of individual members are used by the majority of the group to represent its own hidden resistance to the therapist. In a seventh paper (1985) Rosenthal presented a comprehensive approach to the phenomenon of resistance in group psychotherapy.

CHAPTER 3

Modifications
of Resistance

One of the premises of this chapter can be illustrated by the following vignette from a session of an adult therapy group.

Mark, age 29, had repeatedly complained about his parents, girlfriend, employer, and the teachers in his graduate school (where he was not doing the assigned papers). Norma, a 43-year-old-divorcee who had consistently supported Mark in the group, addressed him with intensity.

"Mark, I've been with you here for two years and I've usually felt very sympathetic towards you, but I've just realized how you misuse this group. You come here to complain about all the injustice in the world, but you're not doing anything else—you haven't got your sights set on anything higher. Your complaints are your whole life. You're just going nowhere, man. If I'm in this group ten years from now, I'm afraid I'll still hear you complaining about the same old things, and you'll probably be exactly where you are now."

The resistances of individual members that emerge in groups are essentially the same—and are as diverse and far-flung—as those that arise in individual therapy. Some are brought into sharper focus and are more visible in the group setting: monopolization, instigation of dissension, the need to scapegoat or be scapegoated, the need to eliminate siblings, and the need to exhibit oneself. The resistances in the two therapeutic settings are similar in nature, but the group endows them with special qualities. One of the unique dimensions that resistance takes on in the group setting is that members deal with one another's defenses and resistances. Bry (1951), in one of the early papers on resistance in groups, noted this aspect. "The first and most striking thing in the handling of resistance is that frequently resistance does not have to be handled at all, at least not by the group therapist. The group itself is remarkably effective in dealing with this phenomenon" (p. 112).

Slavson (1964) addressed this unique quality of the group: "Analytic groups facilitate the acquisition of insights because patients come to grips with resistances, especially defenses and character rigidities, much earlier and in much more telling ways due to the reactions of fellow members than do individual therapy patients" (p. 163). Slavson states that there are inherent solvents of resistance in group therapy and that identification, universalization, and mutual support have the effect of overcoming an individual's defensive resistances.

Several vignettes of actual group-therapy situations illustrate this peer engagement of resistance:

> In the early sessions of a group, Mrs. A. continually advised others on their revealed problems without having made any reference to her own emotional state or difficulties. In the group's fourth meeting, when Mrs. A. again enacted her advisory role, another member turned to her to ask, "Mrs. A., are you the Virgin Mary here? What brought *you* to this group?"

Another example is taken from a mothers' group:

> Mrs. K. had repeatedly expressed great concern and

helplessness in the group about her son's behavior difficulties that kept him constantly embroiled with school authorities. She described his idea of bringing a teacher a "present" of an artificial piece of feces. Mrs. S. exclaimed to Mrs. K.: "And he knows you like the idea!" Mrs. K. reacted with denial, but Mrs. S. continued: "If the corners of your mouth turned up into that smile in front of your son like they're turned up now, he knows that you liked the idea." Mrs. K. grinned and acknowledged that it had been hard for her to keep a straight face. This exchange provided the first opening into Mrs. K's deep need to express her own rebellion through her son.

Frank had come under increasing group scrutiny for his emerging pattern of expressing considerable hostility in an indirect fashion. The group's recognition of this previously concealed aspect of his personality caused growing discomfort in Frank. When he was again faced with everyone but himself perceiving one of his remarks as hostile, Frank withdrew into a sullen and aggrieved silence. Later in the session, he announced that he needed a "rest from the group."

Sid asked sympathetically, "Are we wearing you out?" Frank felt understood by this and spoke of his inability to tolerate the feelings of being constantly misunderstood.

Ina told Frank that he had arrived at a crucial point in his treatment and she couldn't believe he would jeopardize his treatment at this point.

Rachel told Frank, "You're angry. Good. So what's the big deal? We all get angry here and then work it out."

Phil addressed Frank, "You've been asserting yourself lately and so you've made a few mistakes, but what is this nonsense about no one understanding you? The problem is that we are understanding you. Isn't that what you're here for?"

Ina asked, "Frank, do you want to leave here and go back to being the little nice boy that you were a year ago?"

Frank expressed appreciation for the group's help in

preventing him from acting on his feelings and indicated he could not continue to work with the group without threatening to leave whenever he had painful feelings. Frank subsequently told his individual therapist that he was "thrilled" by the group's recognition of the gains he had achieved and by the members' concern for him.

The significance of the above illustrations is that the therapist is not alone in his therapeutic task. He has powerful allies if he is prepared to utilize them and can recognize and accept the fact that other patients may be more effective than he in dealing with certain resistances. Interpretations, observations, and comments directed by the therapist to a group member are frequently perceived as narcissistic injuries; the same comments coming from another group member can be much less toxic and even palatable.

One member's deviousness was focused on by his fellow group members, who told him there was something quite sneaky about the way he related to the group. In an individual session following the group meeting, the patient described reacting with thoughtful self-appraisal to the group's observations and told the therapist, "If you had told me I was a sneak, I would have felt humiliated, and I probably would not have come back. Somehow, coming from them, it didn't hurt and made me think." When the therapist investigated this difference in response to the source of the character analysis, the patient explained, "If you had done it, I'd have felt that my father was out to shame me in front of the whole family."

Thus, the therapist can enlist the assistance of group members in dealing with one another's resistances. Frequently the therapeutic outcome will rest upon his skill in eliciting the members' cooperation in a consistent and planned manner.

The second major characteristic of resistance in the group setting is the trend of group members to function in an organized way, on both conscious and unconscious levels, in relation to the group therapist. This tendency to develop similar libidinal and aggressive strivings, and to behave toward the therapist on the basis of these shared feelings, was recognized by Freud in his 1921 essay on group psychology. This tendency produces group resistance: the sharing of the same resistance pattern by all or a majority of group members.

Some group resistances are readily identifiable—a silent group, a scapegoating group, a group mired in chitchat, or one that remains fixed in one emotional area, (such as a focus on members giving one another advice on their reality situations). A typical classic group resistance is that of not sharing time democratically, shutting out quieter members, or permitting monopolization. Another common group resistance is that of focusing only on the therapist, with the members ignoring one another or consistently minimizing one another's contributions. The reverse—consistently ignoring the therapist—would also constitute a shared resistance.

Some groups may demonstrate a total absorption in their own personal problems, with little or no interest in the difficulties of the others. Again, the opposite may also appear—members plunging in to help one another, avoiding attention to and work on their own problems. Some groups develop a pattern of verbally assaulting one another; others banish all negative feelings and function as mutual-admiration societies. In one group, the expression of sexual feelings may be conspicuously absent; in another, talk of sex for purposes of titillation may be rampant. Some groups may show signs of resistance by straggling in late to sessions, having extragroup social and sexual contacts, or passing out candy, gum, or food to one another in sessions.

The foregoing manifestations of group resistance are all readily identifiable. There are others, however, that can frequently go undetected. Ormont (1968) noted that group resistance that is expressed as mutual hatred or love directed toward the therapist is relatively simple to recognize. What is more frequently encountered, and often unrecognized, is a type of resistive phenomena that functions to avoid adherence to the terms of the group agreement. This resistance is operative whenever the group ignores, tolerates, or subtly or overtly encourages a violation of or departure from the therapeutic contract by one or more of its members. "The deviant member expresses the resistance overtly, the condoning members covertly. The deviant member is allowed to continue on his aberrant way unchallenged because he nakedly plays out the veiled attitudes of the rest of the members" (pp. 1–2).

In his book, Ormont gives the example of the group's prolonged use of a witty actor, whose jokes and flippant remarks provided a shield against painful examination of their feelings. Other examples of this less obvious form of group resistance would be group tolerance, acceptance, or encouragement of a member's lateness, absence, nonpayment of fees, monopolization, or silence.

Ormont's definition of group resistance focuses on a crucial element in the recognition and identification of resistance, namely, the contract. It is the contract that provides the setting and backdrop for the resistance and the field within which it operates.

A variety of group modalities have evolved to meet the needs of varying patient and client groups: guidance groups for patients; homogenous groups of addicts, alcoholics, spouses of alcoholics; groups for the terminally ill; and many others. In each of these, the contract may be different. One group may encourage the bringing of refreshments to sessions. Another, like Alcoholics Anonymous, may see outside contacts among group members as vital adjuncts to the group task. Another may use physical contact among members to achieve therapeutic goals.

The essentials of an analytic contract involve the following:

1. Each member telling, in an emotionally significant manner, the story of his life, including the dimensions of past, present, and plans for the future.
2. Each member taking his share of the total talking time and helping his fellow members do the same.
3. Discussing plans for major life changes before arriving at decisions or acting upon them.

4. Refraining from acting out. This includes such behavior as breaking the confidentiality of the group, indulging in orally gratifying acts during group sessions, engaging in physical rather than verbal communication with fellow members, and engaging in extragroup relationships with other members.

The knowledgeable group therapist does not expect members to be able to live up to the terms of the contract; he expects, and is prepared for, deviations. He is alert to the inevitability of individual, subgroup, and group resistance, and to the probability of a deviant member being the instrument of, and the spokesman for, the resistance of the group when his deviation goes unchallenged or unquestioned.

If unaware of the factor of group gratification and sibling support for the nonconforming member, the group therapist may find himself engaged in a generally futile attempt to deal with an apparent individual resistance, when actually a powerful group resistance is operating.

ILLUSTRATIONS OF GROUP RESISTANCE

In a fathers' group in a child-guidance clinic, Ralph, a flamboyant private detective, consistently regaled his fellow members with lurid tales of crimes, adultery, and violence. His son had been brought to the clinic because of conduct problems in school that featured hyperactivity and the incitement of other students to misconduct.

The therapist sought to deal with Ralph's group behavior as an individual resistance by asking the group members if they saw any connection between Ralph's functioning in the group and his son's excited and instigative school behavior. This question seemed to fall on emotionally deaf ears; the therapist met a barrage of support for Ralph.

"Look, his job is the most important part of his life—why shouldn't he talk about it here?"

"If it helps him relax to talk about these things here, then by all means he should keep right on. The way I see it is this will help him be a better father—so go to it, Ralph!"

"Come on, Doc, we're all interested in each other here and we show it by our interest in each other's families, our problems, our jobs. So what's all the fuss about?"

"Can't you take it if we're not talking about our kids every single minute? What's *your* problem?"

"We're here to learn, aren't we? Well, I learn a lot from Ralph about the seamy side of the world that our kids are going into, things that are important for us as fathers to know."

Feeling helpless and defeated, the therapist retreated into passivity. The resistance continued unabated as Ralph resumed enlivening the group with his stories. The process of resolution was set into motion at the subsequent session when the therapist, armed with the recognition that a full-blown common resistance was operating, opened the meeting by asking, "How would you all like Ralph to excite you today?" Over several sessions, repeated interventions addressed to the whole group's gratification through Ralph's stimulating behavior led to dissolution of the resistance.

A serious group resistance in another fathers' group was marked by the fathers' need to remain hopeless in their relations with their children, in their marriages, and in their unsatisfying jobs. This constellation of feeling despair was accompanied by a readiness to expel any member who felt helped or who spoke of deriving satisfaction from some major life area. Any deviation from this underlying group code came under sharp attack. This treatment-destructive resistance was approached by the therapist repeatedly asking what feelings were safe in the group and what feelings were taboo. Several members subsequently recalled bleak and dreary childhoods dominated by depressed, defeated, and hopeless parental figures.

The group's range of acceptable feelings became progressively wider as the therapist conveyed their entitlement to a broad spectrum of emotions.

One therapist had the unhappy experience of a session beginning with one of the woman members, Wanda, taking her chair and refusing to give it up. She said to the group, "Why can't he sit somewhere else?" The male group members, all of whom had had tyrannical fathers, gave quick evidence of their support for this acting-in behavior. One of them laughed excitedly and exclaimed, "This is fun." Another disparaged the therapist's attempt to explore the feelings Wanda was enacting by asking him, "What are you making such a big deal about?" At the time, the therapist was too upset to explore the group's stake in this oedipal-level id resistance.

Another group developed a continuing pattern of socializing outside in subgroups of two. Members called each other for comfort, met for lunch, hugged and kissed each other, and seemed on the verge of having sex. When the therapist pointed out that this was not cooperative behavior, members argued that they had no pleasure in their lives outside the group and that giving up these extragroup contacts would leave them totally alone and deprived. They spoke repeatedly of feeling close to each other, and each one felt an intense wish to be close to one other member. This group was showing that its members would all rather have sex than put up with the frustration of analysis. The resistance continued because, in addition to the members' gratification through this pattern, the group therapist was a vicarious participant. His own wishes for closeness, arising from his experiences in a large family, prevented him from taking the indicated firm stand in the face of this group's defiance.

The following vignette features a resistive pattern of group

members acting in such a way as to be able to blame the group
for not being interested or understanding.

Audrey would convey that she wanted to be left alone, but
she expected the group to magically know when she did
want interest. When the group missed a cue, she accused
them of disinterest and sat in sullen silence.

Myra adopted a superior, critical attitude toward others
in the group. When this evoked negative responses, she
told the group they were a lousy bunch of ingrates who
did not appreciate her superior ability to size them up.

Andrea waited for interest in her to be shown, but then
only talked about her various somatic symptoms. When
the other members inevitably got bored, she accused them
of blatant and insulting disinterest.

Resolution involved repeated interventions to individual
members, as well as to the group, along the lines of, "How do
you plan on not getting what you want today so that you can
decide this is a lousy group?"

Another group tolerantly witnessed a male member kiss-
ing a female member at the end of each session, a
departure from the contract, which emphasized that feelings were to be expressed in words only. The situation led
to a sexual relationship outside the group and the breaking off of treatment by the two lovers. Subsequent investigation of the group's reluctance to scrutinize this subgroup resistance revealed that the members had been
attaining vicarious sexual gratification from the budding
relationship—a group resistance had been operating.

One group expressed its need to defy the therapist by its
tacit approval of a member who insisted on smoking,
chewing gum, taking his shoes off, and putting his feet up
on the coffee table.

THERAPEUTIC APPROACHES TO GROUP RESISTANCE

The identification and conceptualization of these group forces and the development of therapeutic approaches to deal with them were studied and developed by such prominent figures as Redl, Bion, Spotnitz, Ezriel, and Foulkes.

Redl (1948) was one of the first to identify psychological defenses of the whole group against treatment and change that reached "far beyond the scope of individual resistive behavior."

Bion (1948–1951) found groups to be dominated by certain massive emotional states that result in behavior incompatible with their primary tasks. He specified common motivational elements in groups, in the form of three basic emotional states that relate to the group leader. These "basic assumptions," which can be viewed as a classification of major sources of resistance in the group setting, are dependency, flight-fight, and pairing. Bion addressed his interpretations of the "basic assumptions" to the entire group rather than to an individual member on the basis that the effects would be inclusive since each individual shared in the common group assumption and would find the interpretations relevant to some degree.

Ezriel (1950, 1952) sought out group-based phenomena, directing his attention to conflicts that are engendered in members by their unconscious feelings, impulses, and fantasies toward the leader and one another. Each member attempts to manipulate the others and the leader into assuming assigned roles; each wants the group to correspond to his fantasy. Although each member pursues his own private goals and ends (resistances), the impact of these pushes and pulls on other members and the therapist, providing the basis for common group tensions that reflect the unconscious fantasies of all the group members. Ezriel seeks to understand the common group tension and each individual's contribution to it. He thus uses total-group and individual interpretations.

A total-group approach of group analysis was evolved by Foulkes (1946, 1957), who presented a concept of the group as a mental matrix comprising all the interactions of individual group members that merge into a unified structure. Foulkes (1957) advances the principle that "every event even though apparently confined to one or two participants, in fact involves the group as a whole. Such events are part of a gestalt configuration, of which they constitute the foreground whereas the background is manifested in the rest of the group" (p. 43). The group is seen as having the equivalent of the psychoanalytic states of consciousness and unconsciousness and as showing in its behavior the equivalent of the defense mechanisms. Thus, isolation occurs in a group when an individual is assigned characteristics that are shunned in a phobic way by the others. Foulkes states:

> The group associates, responds and reacts as a whole. The group avails itself now of one speaker, now of another, but it is always the transpersonal network which is sensitized and gives utterance, or responds. In this sense we can postulate the existence of a group "mind." [1957, p. 51]

Foulkes (1957) declares that group analysis recognizes the basic psychoanalytic concepts of transference, unconscious mind, defense mechanisms, resistance, and all the individual dynamics known from psychoanalysis. "None of these are lost or devalued because people sit around in a circle. All these basic ingredients are simply modified by their operation in a group situation" (p. 34). Foulkes contends that the therapist will avail himself of the "new therapeutic weapons" available to him in the group setting. Thus, "interpretations in the group are not individually based but group based. They take regard of, and are directed towards, that group, even if addressed to an individual, and they are continually, like any other communication, of a multi-dimensional, multi-personal effect" (p. 35).

Whitaker and Lieberman (1964) share the view of Bion, Ezriel, and Foulkes that wishes and fears of group members evolve into group-shared unconscious conflicts and themes. They postulate the conflict as being between a disturbing motive (impulse) and a reactive motive. The group's efforts to resolve the conflict result in the group solution. Whitaker and Lieberman identify group themes as a series of focal conflicts centering around a single disturbing motive. These are similar to Bion's basic assumptions, in that they are described as dealing with dependency, aggression, and sex.

Johnson (1963) also espoused an approach geared to the group. In this model, the therapist avoids making interpretations to individual members and seeks to elicit group responses only. Members are encouraged to make their own interpretations to one another. Individual contacts between therapist and group members are discouraged, and those that do occur are brought to the attention of the group. In addition, the group therapist does not have group members as individual patients.

The conceptual and technical approach to the whole group is exemplified in a statement by Bion (1948–1951), who indicates that he used to be seduced into directing interventions to individual members, as in individual analysis. In allowing himself to make individual interventions, the therapist is not only conveying an interest in doing individual therapy in the group setting, but is being influenced by basic-assumption dependency, thus reinforcing the idea that the group consists of a doctor surrounded by dependent patients.

CONFLICT OVER TOTAL-GROUP CONCEPTS

Group-oriented therapists accord a central theoretical and methodological emphasis to total-group concepts. The theories of those emphasizing total-group phenomena are by no means uniform, but they are convinced that the psychotherapeutic group is a unique interpersonal setting. They are convinced that the therapist's understanding and interpretation of group-as-a-whole phenomena furthers the development of all individual members. They maintain that membership in a group evokes shared conflicts and motivations, and they claim that the therapist, by addressing such shared group concerns, may effectively treat each member of the group. In perceiving the group as a unit, these writers tend to ascribe to it such person-based concepts as "group ego" (Mann), "group super-ego" (Semrad and Arsenian), "group tension" (Ezriel), "group resistance" (Spotnitz), and "group focal conflict" (Whitaker and Lieberman).

The emergence of these approaches touched off a long-standing controversy in the field of group psychotherapy. On one side were those who saw group therapy as the application of individual-therapy principles and practices to the group setting. In the other camp were those who were concerned with the utilization of group-specific forces and processes that facilitated treatment.

In the lead article of the first issue of the *International Journal of Group Psychotherapy*, Slavson (1951) drew attention to the conflict: "The placing of primary focus on treatment of the group as a unitary entity, rather than on individual patients, is a development which may prove to be a major crisis" (p. 12). These views, Slavson noted, are reflected in such terms as "group emotion," "group symptom," "group resistance," and "group formation." He seriously questioned whether person-ality problems "can be rectified by the treatment of groups as groups rather than correcting the imbalance of psychic forces in the individual" (p. 12).

In another paper, Slavson (1957) forcefully disputed the idea of common forces in the group: "Each patient seeks to achieve his own aim as an individual for his own individual ends and not for the benefit of the group as a unit or for the sake of a common group aim" (p. 133).

Wolf (1949–1950) cautioned against approaches to group-wide phenomena: "The therapist must be careful not to gen-eralize too broadly from one member to another. A collective interpretation tends to obscure specific differences that vary with each individual and helps the therapist to avoid deeper and more refined interpretation" (p. 147).

McCormick (1957), like Slavson, saw group and individual therapy as utilizing the same processes and sharing the same focus on the individual. Referring to the view holding that the group is the central focus of treatment as the "group dynamics" approach, McCormick asserted that it fell outside the realm of classical psychotherapy by virtue of its group orientation: "Having a different orientation with respect to the dynamics of the therapeutic process, group dynamics practitioners do not recognize the identity of process in individual therapy and in group therapy" (p. 107). They are treating groups essentially, and not individual disturbances and illnesses.

Wolf and Schwartz (1971) emphatically renounced the groupwide orientation, arguing that by directing interventions to the group, the therapist is leading them "toward a uniformity of pathology and away from the wholesome reality of human diversity" (p. 48).

In this same paper, Schwartz and Wolf offer varied explanations for the behavior and motivations of the group-oriented therapists: "A blind but misconceived faith in democracy in which equality is confused with sameness" (p. 142); "the therapist's wish to avoid involvement in the multiplicity of individual problems" (p. 142). They continue:

> An attempt to find a short-cut in group therapy and evade the necessity for detailed, specific, and differentiated analysis of the individual and his problems. Some therapists inappropriately look to this or that patient to be an auxiliary therapist. The group psychodynamicist may be looking to the group itself as an auxiliary therapist, hoping that somehow group activity will therapeutize the individual, without any particular exploration of his unconscious pathology. [p. 142]

The same authors also speculate that an interest in the group as an entity may be a defensive reaction to the analyst's doubts about group therapy. "How better to vindicate group processes than by simply asserting their absolute superiority to individual psychodynamics and thereby gaining unchallengeable certainty. Let us be less defensive rather than more group dynamic" (Wolf and Schwartz 1971, p. 143).

Yalom (1970) attested to the existence of the controversy: "Among various schools of group therapy, the issue of total group interpretations versus interpretations involving a smaller unit or a single member is a highly controversial one; indeed some group therapists make only total group interpretations while others never or rarely do" (p. 129). Yalom then goes on to seriously question the degree of emphasis placed upon concern with the concept of the group. He attributes responsibility to psychoanalysts who brought their terminology with them when they entered the field of group therapy: Concepts such as "group ego" and "group superego" were formulated, with the group seemingly regarded as an autonomous entity.

Yalom decries the tendency to anthropomorphize the group and suggests that it offers conceptual pitfalls. "How do we know what is the dominant group culture, common group tension, or group mind? How many of the group members must be involved before we conclude it is the 'group' speaking?" (p. 130).

Parloff (1968), in a review of significant trends in the field, recognized the continuing existence of the controversy involving the dynamic interaction between two contrasting beliefs regarding the role of the group in the treatment of the individual. These are: (1) the application of the theory and practice of individual treatment in the group setting; and (2) "the identification, development and utilization of forces and processes indigenous to groups to facilitate treatment" (p. 496).

Rosenthal (1978) empirically validated the presence of individual and group orientations among group therapists in the New York metropolitan area. He found that those therapists identified as individual-oriented tended to direct their interventions to the resistances of individual members, whereas group-oriented therapists tended to deal with the common resistances and themes in the group.

HANDLING INDIVIDUAL AND GROUP RESISTANCE

An additional dimension to understanding and managing resistance in group therapy is the therapist's orientation and readiness to recognize and deal primarily with individual resistance or group resistance.

The current approach to dealing with resistance in groups recognizes that individual and group resistance are present throughout the life of the group and that each requires attention. This view also takes into account the dynamic interplay of individual and group in the development and maintenance of resistive operations. A member who persists in lateness or thwarts efforts to seriously explore members' problems may be expressing the covert defiance of the whole group. The group's tolerance and tacit approval of behavior that deviates from their working agreement are an indication that the misbehaving member is the spokesman for the group's resistance.

Individual and group resistance can be simultaneously operative and dynamically interconnected. A majority of members, or a whole group, may be enacting the same resistance, or one or several members may enact a resistance for the group. In the earlier stages of group formation, a variety of individual resistances is usually present. At times the therapist may address both the individual and the group-shared aspects of the resistance. Where a member has maintained silence and has been ignored by the group, the therapist may ask, "How come you are all neglecting Frank, and why is he cooperating in this neglect?"

However, the system of priorities dictates that where a choice is available, the therapist chooses to deal with group resistance first, since he is then treating all the members. In the area of technique, an approach intended for the whole group may give the appearance of an individually oriented intervention when it is directed to the individual who symbolizes or represents the group's resistance.

Individual and group manifestations of resistance appear and disappear in the course of group psychotherapy. The analytic group therapist deals with all resistance, since it is resistance resolution that achieves ameliorative change. When given the opportunity, the therapist seeks to resolve group resistance first, so that maturation can be facilitated in several individuals simultaneously. At the same time, in studying and preparing to deal with a group resistance, the group therapist attempts to understand and reconstruct for himself the origins and function of this particular aspect of resistance in the life history and psychic economy of each member.

Resistance in Group Psychotherapy

The preceding chapter described how the group setting endows resistance with unique dimensions. However, resistance in the group is intrinsically similar to resistance in individual therapy, and the classification of resistance offered by Freud (1926) in *Inhibitions, Symptoms and Anxiety* can be usefully applied.

EGO RESISTANCE

Ego resistance, which appears prominently in the early stage of group treatment, is frequently manifested by objections to disclosing information about some area of life experience. A member may refuse to talk about sex, claiming it is too personal and intimate and therefore no one else's business. Or a member, several members, or the whole group may insist on doing something in violation of the group agreement. Some subcategories of ego resistance are (Ormont 1977):

1. *Negation.* The group demonstrates a negative attitude toward the therapist's wishes to have the group operate

cooperatively. One group refused to talk to the therapist; another maintained lengthy silences.
2. *Limit setting.* A member circumscribes his communications (e.g., "I'll talk about anything here except my sex
life. If anyone mentions sex, I'm leaving.").
3. *Ego protecting.* A member cannot talk about a certain
part of his life, for example, being engaged in some
illegal activity or belonging to a radical group and being
fearful of divulging it.
4. *Subject specialization.* One member participated only
when the subject of men came up, at which time she
would immediately talk about her boyfriend. When the
subject changed, she would disengage again.
5. *Reality focusing.* Some individuals or groups insist upon
a focus on "reality," dismissing fantasies, wishes, and
dreams by continually asking, "What has that got to do
with reality?"

Ego resistances supply valuable insights into the early training members received from their parents. These resistances
respond favorably to acceptance and adjoining, rather than to
corrective efforts. One group, as spring approached, wanted to
have "just one session" for a picnic meeting in the park. The
therapist asked what part of the park they preferred and where
they would sit. He pointed out that park benches would not
permit them to sit in a circle, and asked if they would like to
bring chairs or sit on the grass. As all these possibilities were
raised by the therapist, interest in the once burning issue
waned. Ego resistances, originating in the ego's early developmental stages, are frequently based on the assumption that
others want what the individual wants. They operate as a
defense against anxiety.

In another example of ego resistance, a group of 15-year-
old boys displayed strong reluctance to discuss their
feelings and problems. They preferred to talk about sports
and repeatedly complained that group sessions were
boring and uninteresting. When asked what would make

the sessions more interesting to them, the boys clamored for the addition of girls to the group and couches to replace the chairs.

The group therapist indicated that the suggestion was worthy of consideration. For the next several sessions, the therapist elicited discussion on the possibility of girls joining the group. What kind of girls did they want? What would happen if two group members liked the same girl? What if the girls did not like sports? What would happen to the group therapist's reputation and job if he permitted the group to be turned into a sex club? What would happen if Ralph, who had boasted of taking away his friends' girls, took the girlfriend of another group member?

After thorough discussion of the possible consequences of making the group coed, the boys concluded that bringing in girls would cause more dissention than satisfaction and would probably lead to the breakup of the group. Following this, their craving for excitement subsided and the boys were able to seriously express their feelings about girls, their sisters, and their mothers.

As the therapist studies the group over a period of time, he silently identifies and analyzes emerging resistances. Each is studied to determine its point of origin in the psyche-id, ego, or superego—and the extent of its function—individual, subgroup, or groupwide. The therapist is then in a better position to evaluate the effect of the resistance on the group's functioning and its relative need for attention with respect to other resistances that may be in simultaneous operation. Resolution of ego resistances has the significant effect of smoothing the road toward cooperative group functioning.

SUPEREGO RESISTANCE

The second type of resistance mentioned by Freud, superego resistance, presents attitudes developed in relation to parents during the oedipal period. This type of resistance involves feelings of shame, guilt, embarrassment, and humiliation about disclosing information. This variety of resistance may also express itself in harsh, judgmental, and punitive attitudes toward group nonconformists, as a defense against these critical members' own uncooperative impulses. One group was so persistently moralistic and critical of any perceived moral lapse that the therapist referred to them interpretively as "the should group."

Another form of superego resistance—harsh and punitive self-judgment—may lead some members to feel unworthy of the ameliorative effects of treatment. One man, rejected by his lover, told the group, "I don't deserve her or you." Another group member revealed a pattern of consistently avoiding success. When the group offered suggestions designed to help him overcome some of the reality obstacles in his path, he seemed singularly unable to utilize them. In fact, the group's encouragement seemed to be a source of emotional discomfort to him. At a later stage in his group treatment, he revealed deep feelings of unworthiness, stemming from childhood sexual activity with younger siblings, which permeated his life. In extreme form, such a pattern will operate as a treatment-destructive resistance, and the therapist needs to be alert to the tolerance level of such patients in the areas of acceptance, support, praise, and success.

ID RESISTANCE

Id resistance originates in the unconscious tendency to repeatedly seek some previously experienced gratification—the repetition compulsion. The difficulty in dealing with this resistance resides in its powerful charge of libidinal or aggressive energy. Such gratification, where it becomes a major component of the treatment situation for the individual member or group, is a full-blown id resistance.

Id resistance can express gratification associated with each of the levels of development, and can be predominantly charged by either aggression or libido. An oral-level id resistance might manifest itself in a pervasive libidinal wish to be constantly fed, nurtured, and suckled by the therapist. Behaviorally, this could be expressed by waiting for the therapist to talk, by asking for help, advice, suggestions, and understanding, and by the general adoption of the passive, dependent attitude of the hungry infant. An aggressive id resistance on this level is encountered in the pleasure of making "cutting remarks" with a "biting tongue."

On the anal level, the behavioral equivalents of diarrhea and constipation can be observed in patients who spew out an uncontrolled stream of words or who stingily and spitefully retain their verbal productions, or eke them out only with reluctance and strain. One member would let loose a series of unrelated thoughts and ideas and then sit back with an expression of contentment while the group sought to make sense out of his "mess." Having defecated, he enjoyed being cleaned up and diapered by the group. A delinquent group used several sessions to deluge its therapist with scatological expressions that were accompanied by gales of groupwide laughter. The therapist was left with the clear feeling of having been defecated upon.

On the urethral level, a group of young men constantly competed among themselves in dress, seeking to outdo one other in style and in being sartorially current. They also competitively compared the size of their biceps, and one member claimed superiority over his group rivals in penile dimensions.

On the genital level, these resistances are manifested by attempts to break up any interacting couple in the group and to entice other members (or the therapist) into love relationships. The powerful charge of sexuality from the oedipal period can lead to sexual acting out among group members. Freud (1921) noted that the enactment of directly sexual impulses among members has a disintegrative effect on groups, and experience has borne out the validity of this warning. Id resistances are frequently the cover for hatred and murderous feelings disguised in seductive behavior. One man's constantly charming behavior toward the women in the group cloaked his wish to destroy the male therapist and have the female members to himself.

The therapist's essential approach to id resistance is to constantly educate the group, from the very start, that group psychotherapy involves talking, not action. The statement, "This is a talking group only," bears frequent repetition. The therapist will also investigate and bring under analytic scrutiny those feelings that cause members to make fists, touch each other, bring food to sessions or chew gum, take off their shoes, cry instead of talk, run out of the meeting room, or seek extragroup contact with each other. When the group members accept this basic principle of "talk rather than action," they will recognize acting-in and acting-out behavior as uncooperative.

SECONDARY-GAIN RESISTANCE

In secondary-gain resistance, concealed pleasure, some special benefit, or an advantage is obtained from one's illness and its continuation, or from some exploitation of the treatment situation. This resistance is often clearly observed in the terminal stages of treatment, when members seek to maintain any perceived emotional benefits accruing to them from their illnesses. They will seek to retard, defer, impede, and delay cure and improvement. It is at this time in treatment that old symptoms reappear in an effort to fend off termination.

A whole group may remain helpless and demonstrate powerful status quo resistance so that its members may continue to have the gratification of group membership. This resistance may show itself through concealed exhibitionistic pleasure in talking about sexual matters in a seemingly cooperative fashion. Conversely, a member's seemingly sincere interest in the sexual feelings of fellow members may conceal the gratification of voyeurism. Some members remain silent in order to derive the secondary gain of being courted to participate. This variety of resistance is also visible in patients whose recovery from illness would result in eligibility for military service.

Another form of secondary-gain resistance is operative when

patients avoid disclosing some gratifying activity, such as a perversion or extramarital affair, because of fear that group disapproval might lead to pressure to give up the activity. Secondary-gain resistance is often puzzling to the therapist because group members do not talk about it, but rather act surreptitiously to extract pleasure or gain from the therapeutic situation. Resolution involves bringing this underlying stratum of pleasure into view in the group, then transforming it—by recognition, investigation, and exploration—from a hidden benefit to an overt and analyzable gratification.

In learning to communicate positively as their resistances are resolved, group members become cooperative, functioning members of the group and of society, rather than individuals who are immobilized by their passivity or functioning dangerously by acting on their anger.

The resolution of resistance is as essential to cure in group therapy as it is in individual treatment. The resolution of the resistances of a group provides the same maturational impetus for the group as it does in the treatment of an individual, where the successful handling of resistance lifts the patient to a higher level of development.

TRANSFERENCE RESISTANCE AND GROUP ANALYSIS

The fifth and most fundamental resistance is transference resistance, which holds the key to a cure for the group. Fenichel (1945) states, "The repetition of previously acquired attitudes toward the analyst is but one example of this most significant category of resistance" (p. 29). Freud (1905, 1912, 1914) noted that transference phenomena are the source of the greatest resistances, as well as the most potent instrument for psychoanalytic therapy. Greenson (1967) described transference reactions as "a repetition of the past, a reliving without memory" (p. 182), which is invariably associated with resistance. "On the other hand, the reactions to the analyst provide the most important bridges to the patient's inaccessible past. Transference is a detour on the road to memory and to insight, but it is a pathway where hardly any other exists" (p. 182).

Over the years, doubts have been raised as to whether psychoanalytic therapy—reaching and resolving unconscious conflicts—can be achieved and conducted in groups. A pivotal issue has been that of transference, the twin cornerstone with resistance in psychoanalytic theory, with specific reference to the transference neurosis.

Freud used the term *transference neurosis* in two different ways. One designated a group of neuroses (conversion hysteria, compulsion neurosis, and anxiety hysteria) that were accessible to analysis and in which a therapeutic alliance was possible. The second, and more common usage, referred to neurotic phenomena that are mobilized by the analysis and which, in effect, replace the original neurosis.

Greenson (1967) states that, clinically, the development of the transference neurosis is signaled by an upsurge in the emotional charge of the patient's interest in the analyst and in the analysis. As the patient becomes increasingly preoccupied in this direction, the analyst and the analysis become the preeminent concerns in the patient's life. "Not only do the patient's symptoms and instinctual demands revolve around the analyst, but all the old neurotic conflicts are remobilized and focus on the analytic situation" (p. 188).

Greenson adds that the classical psychoanalytic attitude is to facilitate transference neurosis's maximal development, and that "It is recognized that the transference neurosis offers the most important instrumentality for gaining access to the warded-off past pathogenic experience. The reliving of the repressed past with the analyst is the most effective opportunity for overcoming the neurotic defenses" (p. 190). Thus, the transference neurosis differs form the transference, in that the behavior replacing the earlier neurotic picture is more pathological, more extensive, and more coherent.

SKEPTICS OF GROUP ANALYSIS

Kubie (1958), a respected figure in psychoanalysis, evinced considerable skepticism toward analytic group psychotherapy. Kubie summarized the essence of individual therapy as an attempt to overcome the barriers between unconscious and conscious processes; as a working with transference, resistances, facts, fantasies, and dreams through the investigative process of free association; and as an occurrence in a dyadic setting, in which one remains as unknown as humanly possible so the patient can project upon the analyst all of his fantasies. "The analytic chamber maintains a constancy comparable to that which we create in any experimental procedure so that any variables which are introduced into the interactive will arrive predominantly from the patient" (pp. 8–9). Kubie compares this highly controlled and insulated treatment situation with "the tangled skein of interaction" that results from the multiple transference situation in the group. This contrast leads Kubie to ask about the effect of "such a splintering and diffusion of transference on the ability of each individual to communicate significant material and to relive his crucial early identifications" (p. 17).

Kubie concludes, "The group presents us with a kaleidoscopic picture of innumerable and concurrent variables" and states that "the recognition of the unconscious processes in group members and the communication of those insights with the individuals in the group seems fraught with obstacles which appear almost insuperable" (p. 19).

Locke (1966) noted the following theoretical objections to the idea that psychoanalysis can be conducted in groups: (1) If there is no couch, there is no free association; if there is no free association, there is no psychoanalysis. (2) The group lacks "depth." (3) The transference neurosis cannot be developed or worked through. (4) There is no systematic analysis of resistance.

Greenson (1967) declared, "Psychoanalysis is the only form of psychotherapy which attempts to resolve the transference reactions by systematically and thoroughly analyzing them. In some briefer or diluted versions of psychoanalysis one does so only partially and selectively" (p. 35).

SUPPORTERS OF GROUP ANALYSIS

In response to Kubie, Foulkes (1957), a spokesman for the group-based orientation in group psychotherapy, explored whether the group should be used to communicate insights to individual members about their unconscious. "In my view of group psychotherapy, it should not be so used. The group has a different approach to the unconscious; deliberate interpretations by the leader or anyone else directed to any one individual, are not its stock in trade" (p. 52). Foulkes delineated his approach as geared to treating the group's verbal and nonverbal productions as the group's equivalent to free association. Thus, the sequential flow of the statements, utterances, and postures of the individual members are viewed from the same investigative analytic stance as are the productions of the analysand on the couch.

In his response to Kubie, Grotjahn (1953) replied that insights into the unconscious may be rendered by group members, by the therapist, or by the patient himself. "While the therapist and his assistants in the group may not have all the necessary unconscious material gained from free association, dreams and genetic material about every group member, feeling perception, interpretation and analysis of resistance is ongoing within the group treatment situation" (p. 28). Grotjahn maintained that transference analysis is possible in groups and that "groups, theoretically at least, may approximate the therapeutic effectiveness and scientific validity of psychoanalysis proper" (p. 28).

Eight years after the publication of Kubie's remarks, Durkin (1964) noted the questions he had raised and responded to them:

The analytic group therapist's position is based on Freud's definition of the therapeutic processes as the analysis of transference and resistance in bringing unconscious material to consciousness. In Kubie's view the techniques of free association and so-called analytic situation are also integral parts of the process. [p. 133]

Durkin argued that it is this "unnecessary" fusing of the essential process with the technical procedures that gives rise to Kubie's appropriate doubts as to whether this could take place in groups. She then proposes to simplify the problem by adhering to Freud's definition of the analytic process while at the same time maintaining separation between the nuclear process and the techniques that had been developed for its use in the individual treatment setting. The problem would then be to determine "what changes must be made in the technical procedures so that the process per se will be effective in the group and yet not do violence to its basic nature" (p. 133).

Durkin then refers to Fenichel, who echoed Freud's statement that analysis involves working with transference and resistance. Fenichel (1945) stated: "Whether the patient lies down or sits, whether or not certain rituals of procedures are used, does not matter. That procedure is best which provides the best conditions for the analytic task. *A non-classical procedure, when the classical one is not possible, remains psychoanalysis*" (p. 573).

Noting that neither Freud nor Fenichel insisted upon a fixed mode of implementing the analytic process, Durkin (1964) states that "freed from the limitations of a particular technique (free association) and of a 'scientifically controlled' analytic situation, the outlook for achieving analysis in a group situation is more encouraging" (p. 134).

Durkin is firm in stating her conviction that it is legitimate to speak of transference and transference analysis in group psychotherapy: "We have good reason to insist that in the group the past is restored in the present in all its crucial aspects, that a systematic attack can be made on the resistances and that a resolution of the neuroses does occur to the end of bringing about structural change" (pp. 139–140).

EFFECTIVENESS OF GROUP ANALYSIS

The questions of the legitimacy of group psychotherapy as an effective form of analytic psychotherapy, its capacity to evoke and resolve transference, and its relation to individual psychoanalysis have been addressed by various writers.

Wolf (1949–1950) stressed the analysis of transference in his formulation of psychoanalysis in groups: "The analysis of transference is the largest single area of group concentration" (p. 535). Rather than seeing transference limited in any way by the group setting, Wolf views it as extending the scope and reach of transference through the multiplicity of transference objects available in the group. Wolf, in fact, reverses the usual trend and sees the individual setting as putting "some limitation on the depth of the therapeutic process when the therapist may not elicit multiple transferences. If treatment constitutes primarily the analysis of transference, is it not wiser to place the patient in a group setting in which he can project father, mother and siblings as well?" (p. 18).

In his 1964 text on group psychotherapy, Slavson specified the dilution of the transference as a singular modification of transference phenomena in the group setting. The effects of this dilution are felt in the reduction of the intensity and emotional charge of transference, thus diminishing the intensity of the treatment. This, according to Slavson, prevents deep regression and the emergence of many fantasies which would become available through a more involving treatment such as psychoanalysis. "This, together with other factors renders groups unsuitable for treating massive psychoneuroses" (p. 130). On the other hand, Slavson (1964) and Spanjaard (1959) stressed the singular significance of identification in groups, where multiple transferences provide multiple models and objects of identification.

It is interesting to note that various writers, including Slavson, have tended to view the splitting of the transference in group psychotherapy as a distinct disadvantage. However, Slavson, in an earlier work (1950), listed some of the singular advantages of the diluted transference:

1. It is especially helpful to those who feel guilt and disloyalty to parents and spouses when they are on the verge of developing a strong attachment to an individual therapist. For these, group therapy is considerably less threatening and guilt provoking.
2. It is helpful for those with homosexual trends who are

highly anxious about involvement with a therapist of the same sex.

3. It is helpful for those who have been so hurt and deprived in their earliest relationships that they are extremely fearful of emotional attachment.

Slavson concludes that although transference dilution diminishes the depth of treatment, many patients derive definite advantage from it.

Jackson (1962) affirmed the effective depth of group psychotherapy, in that group members develop transference neuroses as they regress to oedipal and preoedipal levels and form libidinal ties with one another and the therapist. The motivating force in the formation of the transference is seen as the need for each patient to reenact his childhood family. Noting that in individual therapy the patient projects one internalized parent picture at a time, Jackson suggests that a therapy group offers a triangular setting that activates the rivalry of familial conflict, in addition to one-to-one relations. "Consequently, a group member transfers aspects of both parental images simultaneously. In group therapy the transference neurosis is composed not only of projections but each member additionally induces other members to play desired or needed roles. By acting for each other they re-enact the primordial family in the unconscious" (p. 54). Jackson adds that when the individual member is ready to enter the transference neurosis, he unconsciously perceives the whole group as Mother and the therapist as Father. Resistive aspects of the tranference neurosis are cited, i.e., patients often separate internalized parental figures into good and bad. In the group setting, the therapist may represent a bad parent to be defeated, while the group as a whole is the good parent to be pleased.

Jackson suggests that the choice between individual and group therapy should be determined by how each setting structures the transference neurosis, since different settings activate different conflicts. Thus, a given patient's resistances will be stronger in one setting than in another. Jackson concurs with Slavson on the advantage of the group's diluted transference situation for certain patients.

Spotnitz (1961a) recommends combined individual and group psychotherapy as preferred treatment for the psychoneuroses and as superior to individual treatment alone. He sees the group as giving the psychoneurotic patient "family prototypes with whom he can experience a new edition of his infantile conflict—in brief, his need to be loved by both parents and to be free to love them and hate them" (p. 6). He points out that the group experience tends to arouse those conflicts the patient lived through from the ages of 3 to 6. "The inappropriate attitudes and behavior which the group situation opens up to fruitful inspection and interpretation may have been displayed only pallidly in years of individual treatment" (p. 6). Spotnitz suggests that an important consideration in the group treatment of the psychoneurotic is whether the group setting will facilitate sufficient regression for the recapitulation of the infantile conflicts. He indicates that the group setting "has proven its value in resolving the neuroses of psychoneurotic patients who have already received some individual treatment" (p. 10).

Hulse (1965) discussed the impact of the group on the development of transference and suggested that the group neurosis arises when the members competing for the therapist fail to gain adequate relief and satisfaction for their strong transferential fantasies, which they attach to the therapist. Hulse thus perceives the group setting as bringing about a displacement of transference from the therapist-parent onto other group members.

Scheidlinger (1964) suggested that "on the deeper genetic-regressive level the group entity becomes for the individual the symbolic representation of the nurturing mother" (p. 294).

In summary, transference develops in both individual and group psychotherapy. In intensive individual psychotherapy, transference manifestations focus on the analyst as the object of an intense regressive transference and expose the patient's underlying unconscious childhood conflicts to analysis. In contrast to the intense focusing of transference solely upon the therapist, it is generally agreed that the conditions extant in group psychotherapy significantly alter the manner in which transference is manifested. There is more or less general agreement that these modifications occur in two ways. First, the intensity of the transference toward the therapist is to some degree lessened or diluted. In addition, transference is also directed toward other members of the group, and to the group as a whole, as well as toward the therapist.

The existence of intense transference in the group setting is substantiated by the emergence of powerful and varied forms of resistance arising from the transference.

Transference resistance directed toward the therapist is as manifold in the group setting as in individual analysis. It is frequently enacted through the medium of positive transference. Mann (1951) described this form of transference as having the potential for blocking and keeping in check any direct or overt expression of negative feeling toward the therapist. He notes that positive transference may reach almost unique dimension. The flood of warm feeling may swell to the point where group sessions take on an inspirational character and suggest an "intoxification of the group ego" (p. 142) in relation to an omnipotent parent-therapist.

The same group-transference resistance is also described by Yalom (1975): "The group grants the leader superhuman powers. His words are given more weight and imbued with more wisdom than they possess. All faux pas or errors of the therapist are seen as deliberate attempts to provoke the group for its own good. All progress is attributed to him. . . . " (p. 198). The members believe that there are incalculable, almost mystical depths to the therapist's interpretations and that he unerringly predicts and benignly controls all events in the group. Professions of ignorance, confusion, or weakness of any kind by the therapist are construed to be part of his repertoire of techniques, planfully designed to exert positive therapeutic impact on the group.

One group persisted in seeing its therapist as a great and endlessly giving mother: adoring him, hanging on his every word, regularly maneuvering him to be the constantly feeding parent. If he gave a lecture or spoke at a professional meeting, the group would be there to take in his words with rapt attention. In this behavior, the group was seeking a repetition of the experience with an all-giving mother that they had had for far too brief a period in infancy. At the same time, their idealization of the therapist served as a defense against their disappointment with the mother who stopped giving and the depression which ensued.

A variety of interventions were used by the therapist in the resolution of this strong transference resistance: a classical interpretation of their underlying disappointment and their need to keep the therapist in a constantly feeding position (prefacing his statements with "The giving mother says . . . ") and psychological reflection, wherein the therapist assumed the group's role of the ever-hungry child. In this last strategic approach, the therapist sought help with problems of his own, such as how to deal with a needy individual patient or with a whole variety of problems that might arise in his practice. Repeating his requests for help and putting the group in the position of having to talk enabled the members to openly vent their frustrations, their depressions, and, finally, their aggression against the no longer adored therapist.

Yalom (1970) describes one member who brought a list of issues that troubled him to session after session, waiting for the therapist to divine its existence and ask him to read it. Obviously, if he had really wanted to work on the problems, he would have taken the initiative himself and presented the list to the group. What was of overriding importance to this patient was the need to have the therapist be his all-knowing parent. His transference was such that he had incompletely differentiated himself from the therapist: If *he* knew something, that was tantamount to the therapist knowing and feeling it. The transference resistance operated to prevent him from properly communicating his wishes to the therapist and the group.

Group negative-transference resistance can function in the following manner.

> The members of one group repeatedly conveyed feelings that the group was not the right one for them. They complained that it reminded them of their unhappy families and that other group members were unlikable, unhelpful, unconcerned, and uninterested. Members frequently spoke glumly of not wanting to come to sessions or dropping out. Resolution of this resistance was achieved through investigation, understanding, and analysis of what made the members feel theirs was a "rotten" group. The therapist convinced the whole group to participate in this investigation (which countered this group's tendency to eliminate one or two members by ignoring them). Interventions were directed toward the group: "You all sound gloomy." "You all look morose." "Why are you all ignoring Helen?" At times the group's attention was called to the resistive behavior of one or several of its members.
>
> Investigation elicited the cause of each individual member's negative feelings about the group. Paula thought the group was rotten because it wasn't run the way she wanted it to be run. Sol's disenchantment with the group was a response to Paula's controlling and interruptive behavior, which he found intensely aggravating. Orin, the one nontherapist in the group, felt he wasn't respected by the others. Iris's resentment was based on her feeling that no one in the group cared for her, especially the other women. This represented for her a capitulation to her family configuration, where she was excluded by the intense involvement between her mother and sister. Irving relived his elementary school experience when he took drugs and felt "out of it." Gabriel felt criticized and unliked, a reenactment of his family experience. Lionel

enacted his isolation resulting from a preoccupation with waiting for the father who had abandoned him. When the other members did not "come looking for him" by paying attention to him, he felt the group was not right for him.

One group therapist was hospitalized for minor surgery and cancelled two group sessions. Upon his return, he encountered intense transference resistance manifested by sullen anger and resentment in the whole group and in three particular members being on the verge of leaving. Investigation revealed that Ira, who had never been let in on his family's secrets, felt hurt, humiliated, and betrayed because the therapist had not shared the details of his illness with him. Susan was "disgusted" with the therapist for being "phoney" and "insincere" by telling her that he was feeling fine when she inquired about his condition while he was hospitalized. Susan had transferred onto the therapist all the hurt and fury she had felt with her father, who offered her clichés and bromides rather than genuine feeling. In the therapist's absence, Emily campaigned to have the group meet and socialize at her apartment, thus reenacting her feelings of emotional abandonment when her own father left, and her wish to succeed him in the family.

As noted earlier in this chapter, group members tend to deal with one another's resistance. This phenomenon is also observed in transference resistance. Although a majority of the members may be locked into a pattern of transference resistance (seeing the therapist as a revered or despicable figure) there are usually several members whose emotional vision is clearer, in that they are not caught up in a particular transference stage. These less-conflicted members can be utilized to present a more realistic perception of the therapist, thereby countering the distortions of transference and gradually bringing other members into this more objective subgroup.

An added feature of this most crucial resistance is that it may (and frequently does) encompass components of other forms of resistance. A group-transference resistance with id- and ego-resistive elements is illustrated in the following exchange:

> *Therapist*: You were all talking in the waiting room and now that you are in this room with me, you are silent. What's going on?
>
> *Member A*: To hell with you!
>
> *Therapist*: Why to hell with me?
>
> *Member A*: Just because you want us to talk, we won't do it.
>
> *Member B*: Right on!
>
> *Member C*: You're always so smart! Figure it out for yourself.
>
> *Member D*: (*Grinning with excitement.*) Don't tell him a damn thing.

The preceding vignettes and examples have been presented to illustrate the emergence, development, and resolution of a number of transference resistances on varying developmental levels and in varying gradations of emotional intensity. The group's capacity to elicit, evoke, heighten, and eventually resolve intense transference feelings and the resistances that arise from them validates group psychotherapy as an effective form of analytic psychotherapy. The modern analytic group psychotherapist works with the cornerstone processes of resistance and transference. He seeks to deal with their manifestations on a groupwide level as the resistances and transferences of individual members converge and coalesce into group resistances and group transference. In this framework, and in following the principles of resolution of resistance, the therapist can help to free a group of human beings from the tyranny of unconscious and compulsive impulse patterns they do not comprehend.

CHAPTER 5

The Sequential Approach to Resistance

Another approach to resistance is a sequential one, which reflects the relative urgency of intervention and resolution for a given resistance. This approach embraces five major resistive patterns that can operate as individual, subgroup, or group resistances: treatment-destructive, status quo, resistance to progress, resistance to teamwork, and termination resistance. In this sequence, first priority is accorded to group-destructive and treatment-destructive resistance.

TREATMENT-DESTRUCTIVE RESISTANCE

The group analyst accepts responsibility for maintaining the integrity of the group and preserving it as a therapeutic entity. By its evocation of familial configuration (multiple transferences), the group elicits patterns of accommodation that emerge as resistances. Some surface gradually and can be studied unhurriedly by the group therapist until they develop fully as transferences. Other resistances, such as the need to conceal one's own inadequacy by concentrating on helpfulness to others or serving as "doctor's assistant," pose no danger to group functioning and can await handling by the other group members. However, certain forms of resistance may endanger the integrity of the group or expose a member to potentially damaging contact.

Spotnitz (1969a) has defined treatment-destructive resistance as "any form of non-cooperative behavior which, if permitted to continue, would seriously disrupt the total functioning of the group 'family' or lead to the elimination of one of its members" (p. 212). This category of resistance would include absence without notice, chronic lateness, destructive manifestations of acting out (such as striking another member, refusing to talk, or preventing others from talking), running out of the room, and unexplained and protracted delays in payment of fees.

The need for alertness to these resistances is also noted by Yalom (1970), who emphasizes: "The therapist must recognize and negotiate any factors which foster or portend group dissolution. Continued tardiness, absences, subgrouping, disruptive extragroup socialization, scapegoating—all threaten the integrity of the group and command the intervention of the therapist" (p. 84).

PREMATURE TERMINATION

The extent of one prevalent form of group-destructive resistance—premature termination—is noted by Yalom. He observes that in the normal course of events, 10–35 percent of members drop out in the first 12–20 sessions, and a similar percentage of new additions drop out in the first dozen or so sessions. Johnson (1963) paid particular attention to this problem. He estimated that group losses average between one-third and one-half of the original members, citing a statistical study of eight groups of eight members each in which total losses during one year were 26 patients, or 40.6 percent.

One of the first to address the problem of premature termination was Bross (1956). Discussing the "deserter" in group psychotherapy, she stressed the therapist's role in helping the potential deserter talk about his anxiety: "The role of the therapist is of indisputable importance here. The problems that confront him are: at what particular moment should the patient's anxiety be recognized, and at what point should the therapist intervene to promote verbalization, elicit feelings, and abort the panic that generates the impulse to run" (p. 392).

The conversion of hostile-aggressive impulses into language is the major strategy in the group analyst's campaign to neutralize the impact of treatment-destructive forces. In a paper on resistance in group therapy with adolescents, Rosenthal (1971) states, "The verbal expression of negative affect toward the group is the best possible guarantee against precipitous withdrawal" (p. 358). Spotnitz (1968a) advised that therapists, in the face of group member behavior that threatens the continuation of treatment, should set about dealing with "the forces that interfere with the verbalization of pent-up feeling." (p. 16). Clues to the early recognition of budding premature termination are offered by the following behaviors:

a developing pattern of lateness in a usually punctual member, absence from a session without notice, falling behind in payment without plausible explanation, complaints of being misunderstood, confused or upset by the group, forgetting a session, evidence of decreasing participation, slightly moving one's chair backward and out of the circle, falling asleep in the group, an abrupt cutoff of information about a major life area which the member had previously been willing to discuss. [p. 16]

Ormont and Strean (1978) note that the deadlier forms of this type of treatment-destructive resistance are those that develop silently and insidiously, so the group therapist is not aware of them until a member announces at the end of a group session that he is not returning, or disappears without a word. The authors caution that "silence is always suspect," especially if it seems to be accompanied by discomfort or anxiety.

Prime candidates for premature termination are those who enter group treatment under some form of duress: for example, a spouse's threat to break up the marriage unless the mate undergoes treatment. Such patients may initially demonstrate anxiety about the threatened disruption of a relationship, and they may even profess an initial wish for help. However, such reluctant draftees are frequently awaiting the first opportunity to bolt from treatment.

> Tom entered a group as the result of his wife's urgent complaints about his chronically rejecting treatment of their 19-year-old daughter. He had had a brief group experience 12 years earlier, and was quite vague concerning the details of this experience.
>
> Sensing Tom's underlying negative feelings toward treatment, the therapist introduced him by saying, "This is Tom—you'd all better get to know him fast, because I don't expect him to be around very long." Tom then assured the group that he entertained no plans to leave abruptly. For some sessions the group examined his relationship with his daughter, empathized with his hurt feelings at the cold war between them, and offered suggestions for understanding and dealing with her that Tom indicated he found helpful. After ten sessions, with some easing of the tension with his daughter and at the first sign of his wife's lessened interest in his treatment, Tom abruptly terminated.

Abrupt termination may also be a function of faulty selection and/or preparation of members for group psychotherapy, which results in premature or ill-timed exposure to a group.

> A young group therapist found that a group he had recently formed was dwindling in membership. Anxious about the possibility of the total dissolution of the group, he persuaded a new individual patient, whom he had seen for only two months, to join the group. In response to the abrupt change in the treatment agreement and the disruption of her incipient feelings of trust in the thera-

pist, the patient suddenly withdrew from both individual and group therapy after attending three group sessions. The therapist had unwittingly reenacted a crucial aspect of the patient's life history. This young woman had been thrust into nursery school and group activities before she had established her basic feeling of belongingness in the crucial dyad with her mother, which provides the foundation for subsequent relatedness to groups.

Another therapist enthusiastically presented the advantages of group therapy to a socially fearful patient. When the patient responded with objections charged by her anxiety, the therapist dealt logically with each objection and exhorted the patient, "Try it—you'll like it." The patient fled the group after one session to which she had come forty minutes late.

DESTRUCTIVE AGGRESSION

Premature terminators nullify their own treatment; other forms of destructive resistance threaten the treatment of other members. A blatantly destructive behavioral pattern is reported by Kadis and colleagues (1963) in their description of Stanley, an individual who drove three successive new members out of a group. Upon the arrival of a new member, Stanley would immediately interrogate him about his reasons for wanting group therapy. He would then offer evidence that the group and the therapist could not help the new patient. This barrage created such anxiety that new members fled. When other members tried to stop his behavior, Stanley maintained he was only exercising the privilege of expressing his feelings.

Stanley's behavior illustrates, in extreme form, a resistance in which freedom of expression is misused to gratify murderous impulses. This form of destructive behavior was enacted in another group by Tania. She would hurl a torrent of abuse, avowedly aimed at hurting her victim, at anyone who opposed or criticized her. Under the pressure of the analyst's warning that continuation of this behavior would result in her removal from the group, and in response to the repeated

admonitions of her fellow members that her attacking out-
bursts were inappropriate in group therapy, Tania modified
her behavior. Under the group's patient guidance, she learned
to say, "I feel hurt, and I'd like to hurt you," rather than acting
in on her feelings.

Tania is illustrative of a category of patient who plays an
instigative role in inciting conflict and aggression within the
group. They seem to bend their efforts to foment tension and ill
feeling among members. When it maintains the group in such
a state of tension that the therapeutic climate is seriously
vitiated, this pattern operates as a treatment-destructive resistance. As other members begin to feel that no sustained
discussion or sympathetic recognition of their problems is
likely to occur in this acrimonious atmosphere, the possibility
of departures from the group is heightened. If the instigator
cannot verbally communicate his wish to deprive the therapist
and fellow members of a harmonious and cooperative family,
removal from the group may be indicated.

GROUP DESTRUCTIVE RESISTANCE

The forms and varieties of destructive resistance are many, and
they may occur as individual, subgroup, or total-group phenomena.

> In a newly organized group-therapy seminar in a social
> agency, the agreement was reached that members would
> present problems arising within their groups and would
> help fellow group therapists do the same. At the seminar's
> second meeting, one member presented his problem with
> a frustratingly passive group. He was then subjected to a
> fusillade of personal comments regarding his own passive
> traits, his identification with his father, and his castration
> fears. In the face of this onslaught, his presentation
> halted. This resistance was resolved when the seminar
> leader remarked that the group seemed more interested in
> dealing with one another's feelings than in learning about

group therapy, and that they all seemed to be doing a good job of ensuring that no one else would want to present problems to this group.

Another example of a whole group enacting a treatment-destructive resistance was that of a school group of predelinquent, early adolescent girls who were referred as a unit to a child-guidance clinic. The girls were seen on an exploratory basis by an experienced group therapist. These early sessions were marked by vivid descriptions of perverse sexual acts and acts of sadistic aggression presented in an atmosphere of excitement. It was discovered that group members met before the sessions, to plan a contrived sexual and aggressive agenda designed to shock the therapist. Exploration of the girls' attitudes toward the clinic revealed they had little interest in attaining an understanding of themselves and strong wishes to defeat authority. Group sessions were terminated. Several girls were later able to constructively use individual treatment.

In a group of mothers of disturbed children, two members developed strong reciprocal negative transferences, each perceiving the other as her critical, rejecting mother. Their bitter exchanges dominated the group and kept it in a state of tension. Each bitterly accused the therapist and other members of favoring the other. Each of the combatants tried to blackmail the analyst into eliminating the other through threats: "I'm not talking or listening as long as she's here." After unsuccessful attempts to deal with them as individuals, the analyst addressed the two belligerents as a resistive subgroup, telling them they were both acting in a blatantly uncooperative manner without regard for the treatment needs of other members. Reflecting their blackmail, the therapist warned that if they could not behave more cooperatively, he would have to ask both to leave. With their acting in curbed by the therapist's intervention, each rival was able to remember her intense struggle with her mother and siblings for the attention of her father.

Olivia had attended the group irregularly and had revealed nothing about her personal life. When several of her fellow members questioned her uneven attendance, she stalked angrily out of the room. In subsequent sessions group members, fearing another explosion, avoided contact with her. Olivia's emotional blackmail thus effectively denied other members the right to express their feelings toward her. A sequence of interventions by the therapist was required to loosen this resistance: He asked Olivia if she had any idea why the group was avoiding her and then explored with her what kind of group contact would cause her to stomp out.

DESTRUCTIVE MONOPOLIZATION

Monopolization of the group session by an individual or subgroup can effectively deny treatment to other members.

Ed, a member of a newly formed adult group, would talk on and on about his own feelings and experiences, with no awareness of the obvious restlessness, boredom, and frustration of his fellow group members. Whenever the therapist intervened to ask Ed how he thought the group was reacting to him or how much time he thought each member should have in a session, Ed would shrug and slump into hurt isolation. His marked early deprivation had rendered him unready for the frustrations of group living. In individual treatment after his removal from the group, he recalled constantly stealing food from his siblings at mealtimes. Ed was thus enacting an oral-level id resistance, aggressive type.

Another example of a patient who could not tolerate the frustration of being denied certain gratifications from the group was Frank, a 38-year-old policeman.

Divorced by his wife and rejected by his daughters, Frank was extremely insecure with women. In the group he needed to present himself as fully adequate, firing off prescriptions for self-help to all the other members. He had a special need to have a benevolent big-brother relationship with women he perceived as inadequate and not threatening to him. He persistently pursued this role with Sylvia, the group's most fragile member. In Frank's sixth session, Sylvia expressed feelings of not being understood by Frank and added that his pressuring suggestions made her anxious. Frank responded with contemptuous anger: "You have nothing to offer me—you're useless!" Sylvia cringed under the attack. The therapist intervened by suggesting that Frank express his feelings toward Sylvia, rather than act on them by attacking her. At this, Frank stood up and stated angrily, "I don't need this shit," and stalked out. He did not return to the group.

Frank's exit line suggests that he was not emotionally toilet trained. He could brook no interference with his sadistic impulse to emotionally defecate on Sylvia once she frustrated him. Although it is doubtful that Frank possessed the requisite ego strengths for group psychotherapy, in hindsight, a prophylactic intervention might have been made in his first or second session: "Frank, how long would you remain in this group if people here didn't appreciate your advice and all the help you offer them?"

Monopolization by one or several individuals can operate as a group resistance when a majority of members tolerate, support, or encourage it. One group permitted two members to bicker with each other for prolonged periods until the group analyst began several meetings by asking, "How would you all like Fred and Mary to dominate the group today?"

Group support may also operate in the case of a silent member. The temptation to encourage defiant, uncooperative behavior in others or to encourage a rival to engage in treatment-destructive actions seems irresistible at times.

Nancy, a member of a group of young adults, was unable to attend a session because she had gotten drunk. At the following session, when the group discussed this as undesirable behavior, Henry protested that he saw nothing wrong with it and exclaimed the strong feeling, "If Nancy had called the group to say she wanted to stay out to get drunk, I'd have told her to go right ahead."

Miranda enacted her murderous feelings toward siblings in a group-destructive manner by immediately supporting and encouraging the proposed departure of any member who expressed an impulse to leave the group. Her pattern was brought to the attention of the group in a session when Miranda kept offering a variety of ostensibly helpful rationales for leaving to John, who had questioned whether he should continue. At this meeting the therapist asked the group who among them would be the most disappointed if John were to stay. Later in treatment, Miranda was able to remember how, as the youngest and most neglected child in a large family, she had eagerly awaited the departure of her older brothers and sisters from the home.

DESTRUCTIVE SEXUAL ACTIVITIES

In his essay on group psychology, Freud (1921) observed that sexual love relationships were inimical to the formation and development of groups. This is also true for group therapy, where sexual acting out among the members can seriously endanger group integrity. Yalom (1975) cites clinical experience that demonstrates that when group members become involved sexually, their valuation of and investment in the group diminishes as their involvement in the dyadic relationship is heightened. They refuse to betray each other's confidences, continue to court each other in the group session by being seductive, attentive, and charming and, in effect, cease being helpful to each other. "They live for one another, blurring out the therapist and other members, and, most importantly, their primary goals in therapy. The effects on the other members are equally antitherapeutic. They resent being left out, they resent the amount of energy consumed by the dyad; they are restricted by sexualization" (pp. 79–80). Yalom concludes from his own experience that, with extreme effort, the therapist may extract therapeutic profit from such an event. "However, the process is risky and exacts a high toll from the rest of the group. The therapist does well to heed Freud's warning to discourage sexual love between members of his group" (p. 80).

> Two mutually attracted members of a group met for dinner. The woman had her young son with her, and in the course of the evening, the man criticized the fellow member's handling of the child. She responded with a scathing denunciation of him for interfering in her relationship with her child. The man in turn felt so deeply humiliated that he was unable to return to the group. The woman dropped out shortly afterward, when several group members blamed her for the man's termination. In effect, the two had destroyed each other's treatment.

Alertness by the group analyst can forestall action by mutually attracted pairs by eliciting verbalization of their feelings for each other in the group sessions. As the therapist becomes aware of two members looking at each other with interest and excitement or addressing their remarks primarily to each other, he may bring their relationship under group scrutiny and subject it to prophylactic exploration and analysis: He might ask why John and Mary are more interested in each other than in anyone else in the group.

DESTRUCTIVE DENIAL OF FEELINGS

Group- and treatment-destructive resistance can also be expressed by efforts to limit the right of other members to express their feelings. Immediate intervention by the therapist was necessitated in a group of delinquent girls when one member threatened to beat up anyone who spoke of mothers.

In an adult group, Myra consistently reacted to any display of angry feeling with attempts to deny its intent and efforts to seal off its further expression. Typical of her responses were, "I'm sure you don't mean that about your mother—after all, the poor woman is only doing her best," or "How can you feel that way about a member of your own family? After all, isn't blood thicker than water?" In the face of any expression of negative feelings toward the group therapist, Myra would characteristically offer, "How can you say that about Dr. B. when he's trying so hard to help each of us?" At intervals, Myra would deliver aggression-denying clichés such as "To err is human, to forgive is divine," or prescribe to a depressed member that he or she "Try looking at the happy side of life."

Myra's pattern operated as a treatment-destructive resistance on two levels. First, it blocked one of the group's vital paths of emotional communication. Second, it mobilized intense group hostility toward Myra, which, if permitted to build up, could have resulted in a harmful massive outburst that could have driven Myra out of the group. The intervention that led to Myra's *Pollyanna* resistance becoming emotionally comprehensible to herself and to the group was the therapist's question, "Why doesn't Myra feel that anyone here, including herself, is entitled to angry feelings?" A sympathetic investigation of the origin of this defense was then conducted by the group. Armed with an understanding of how a tragic series of deaths of siblings and parents in Myra's childhood had affected her, group members were then able to deal constructively with her defenses of denial and isolation. They also made her aware that her fear of killing was killing off feelings—her own and theirs.

In its extreme forms behavior like Myra's, in relation to major feeling constellations such as sex, regression, or aggression, can take on a witch-hunting quality that can have a noxious effect on the group therapeutic process and may not be amenable to resolution in group psychotherapy alone.

DESTRUCTIVE GROUP AGGRESSION

A treatment-destructive group resistance in a fathers' group at a child-guidance agency took the form of sharp and probing interrogation at each new member, immediately upon his arrival, concerning his contributions to his child's difficulties. Responses that the group deemed defensive or denying were met with sharp criticism and allegations that the new member was dishonest or blind to his own role in the problem. As a result, a revolving door policy was established, with new members leaving after one or two sessions and the group nucleus of four members maintaining steady attendance. This was the therapist's first group, and he attributed the swift demise of new members to his own faulty selection or to resistance and lack of ego strength on the part of the disappearing patients.

The process of resolving this deadly infanticide resistance began with the therapist finally becoming aware of its existence. He was then able to ask the group what kind of reception they were planning for the next new member. Were they planning to have him survive one session, or possibly two? An uneasy silence followed, broken by one of the fathers asking, "Are we that bad?" The therapist also asked what kind of new member could survive in such a group. Perhaps, he suggested, he had been picking the wrong people for this group. The group then suggested that he select those "who are ready to have their liabilities pointed out."

As a result of this investigation of the resistance, the group's blueprint for dealing with new members emerged in sharp focus. They had a need for incoming members to immediately acknowledge fault and inadequacy. If this admission was not forthcoming, they needed to employ third-degree tactics until the victim submitted or left. Continuing work with the resistance proceeded along the lines of investigating why it was so important to them to have new arrivals acknowledge inadequacy and how it made the group feel when a newcomer did not admit to fault. The members then revealed the dynamics that had sustained the resistance: identification with their own highly critical, interrogating parents; resentment of the new siblings in their own families; envy and fear of other males, "wise guys," who seemed confident and superior, thereby inducing intense feelings of inadequacy in them. With the establishment of a more tolerant view of their own shortcomings and an emotional awareness of how they had been acting on their feelings, the group was able to assimilate new members and deal more acceptingly with their initial defenses.

THE DESTRUCTIVE NEED FOR EXPULSION

One of the most dangerous and difficult of group-destructive resistances is the need to provoke and court expulsion and "murder" by the group. Patients who demonstrate this resistance enter the group avowedly seeking help. They then provoke their fellow members and the therapist to expel them. Frequently this behavior represents a reenactment of expulsion from the patient's very first group—the family. Individuals who present a history of repeated early institutional and foster-home placements can be viewed by the alert group therapist as prime candidates for demonstrating this resistance.

Henry, a member of an activity therapy group of latency boys, had been born prematurely in the sixth month of pregnancy and was miraculously kept alive by incubation. At the time that the case came to the child-guidance agency, the mother complained about his social isolation and significantly presented the issue as, "I want him to go *out* to play, and he wants to stay *in* the house."

In the group, Henry did many things to court expulsion—wantonly destroying plane models he had asked the therapist to obtain for him, defacing a bookcase the therapist was working on, and throwing refreshments on the floor or "accidentally" spilling soda on the therapist. At one point the therapist was sweeping up at the close of a group session and when the dirt was in a neat pile, Henry kicked it around. The therapist reacted angrily with, "Damn it, Henry! Don't you know by now that I'm not going to kick you out of this group?"

Henry seemed very struck with this statement and showed a marked change in behavior from the next session on. He became the protector, preserver, and repairer of the meeting room and its equipment. When another child gouged a hole in the wall, Henry patched it and then told the therapist that the walls were quite strong again. Henry was now symbolically preparing the walls of the womb to hold him for the right amount of time. His blatantly provocative behavior had apparently been communicating the preverbal material of his premature expulsion from the womb and the continuing rejection by his mother.

Another example of the successful use of this resistance (and failure by the therapist to resolve it) is offered:

Yolanda was a successful music therapist in her mid-sixties. She had had many years and varieties of treatment for her serious bouts of depression. In the screening interview she made a highly positive impression on the group therapist with her honesty, insight, emotional openness, vibrancy, and the courage and tenacity of her lifelong struggle with serious emotional problems dating from the traumatic fragmentation of her family at the age of three.

At her initial group session, Yolanda sat quietly for the first half hour as members discussed ongoing problems. She then abruptly exploded with a flood of anger at the group for ignoring her, excoriating the members for their insensitivity to her, and acidly commenting upon the pettiness of the problems they had raised and the stupidity of the solutions they offered one another.

When asked why she hadn't expressed her feelings earlier in the session, her biting response, "You mean I'm supposed to beg you for a little attention?" revealed the infant's wish to have its mind read by the mother and its fury when this was not forthcoming. When several members sought to support Yolanda by attempting to convey their understanding of her anxiety and hurt in a new situation, she turned on them with scorn for coming with "too little, too late." For an hour Yolanda maintained the group in an emotional storm with herself at the vortex. There was an unmistakable air of excitement about Yolanda as she repeatedly hurled her insults and accusations at the group. By the end of the session, she had attained the goal she had so relentlessly pursued—total alienation of the whole group.

An earlier interpretation by the therapist that she seemed to be finding it very exciting to be the center of the group's negative attention achieved a brief smile from Yolanda and a just-as-brief lull in her expulsion-seeking behavior.

The feelings she had aroused were pungently expressed in members' observations that she had come not for treatment but for some kind of sexually gratifying fighting. They felt she was the biggest infant they had ever encountered, an emotional vacuum cleaner sucking up all the attention and energy of the group, and that she was obviously far from ready for group therapy. To everyone's relief, Yolanda did not return to the group.

The prototype for this form of group and treatment-destructive resistance can be found in the biblical story of Joseph. The Bible tells us that Jacob loved Joseph more than all his children, "because he was the son of his old age: and he made him a coat of many colors. And when his brethren saw that their father loved him more than all his brethren, they hated him, and could not speak peaceably unto him" (Genesis 37:3–4).

The foregoing describes the father's group-destructive behavior; now we come to Joseph's: "And Joseph dreamed a dream, and he told it to his brethren . . . And he said unto them, Hear, I pray you, this dream which I have dreamed: For, behold, we were binding sheaves in the field, and, lo, my sheaf arose, and also stood upright; and, behold, your sheaves . . . made obeisance to my sheaf. And his brethren said to him, Shalt thou indeed reign over us? . . . And they hated him yet the more for his dreams, and for his words" (Genesis 37:5–8).

Still unsatisfied, Joseph continues his provocative behavior and intensifies the group's impulses to expel him. "And he dreamed yet another dream, and told it his brethren, and said, Behold, I have dreamed a dream more; and, behold, the sun and the moon and the eleven stars made obeisance to me" (Genesis 37:9).

Joseph's need to induce intense hatred in his brothers – aided and abetted by his father's blatant favoritism – led to his expulsion from the family group and almost resulted in his murder, providing ancient evidence of the dangerous power of this resistance pattern.

CAUSES OF DESTRUCTIVE RESISTANCES

The presence of destructive resistances appears to be related to destructive experiences in the life histories of those who use them. They seem to need to repeat those experiences in the group, as the victim, and to victimize others through identification with the original aggressor.

Joan, a silent group member, indulged in weekend-long solitary drinking, which left her senseless. She courted danger by walking alone to parks late at night. She was raised by a sadistic mother who beat her, repeatedly told her she was unwanted, and prohibited any outside relationships.

Ethel repeatedly invited attack from other group members by her pedantic and critical approach to them. At other times she presented herself as a totally helpless victim. As a child she was the family scapegoat, constantly being told to shut up, and she was continually derogated by her mother (who was herself intensely disliked by members of the extended family).

Dan, a member of a therapy group of preadolescent boys, drove several weaker members out by physical attack, intimidation, and harassment. He continually searched for the weaknesses of other members and then gloated over them and exploited them. Dan was born to a mother who hated him from birth and a father who ceaselessly probed for the weaknesses of everyone in the family.

Ben abruptly terminated his group treatment after his girlfriend returned from a vacation and greeted him unenthusiastically. He blamed the group for having pressed him to become more understanding of her needs, which, he angrily charged, only resulted in his own deprivation. Ben grew up in an unloving family. When he was 4, his mother suffered a postpartum depression that resulted in his being sent to a neighbor's home for a month.

Tania, mentioned earlier for her extreme vituperation, was constantly threatened with placement and at age 8 was locked in the cellar and told that rats would eat her.

MINIMIZING DESTRUCTIVE BEHAVIOR

Understanding the individual's toxic experiences during his crucial developmental years alerts the group analyst to predictable patterns of destructive resistance. Knowledge of the life histories of prospective group members is essential to developing a group with the potential for cooperative functioning, so the therapeutic process will operate for the emotional benefit of all members.

Group analysts have no immunity from destructive wishes toward their groups, and the enactment of these impulses may include any of the following: forming blatantly ill-suited groups that are bound to disintegrate; permitting destructive behavior; avoiding setting a group agreement that defines what constitutes desirable and cooperative behavior; permitting the group to dwindle without adequately replenishing it; permitting abrupt and repeated absences; seducing members into individual contacts; rejecting every potential group member in the screening process. The cumulative impact of the emotional stimulation to which the group therapist is exposed – the feelings of each member toward him and toward one another, and his own countertransference toward each member and toward the group as a whole – combines to seriously test his disciplined capacity to feel those feelings and act in appropriate therapeutic fashion.

Following are guidelines for minimizing group- and treatment-destructive behavior:

1. Control the degree of excitement and stimulation to which patients in group therapy are exposed, in order to avoid an intense or sudden mobilization of feeling that cannot be adequately released in words. This may necessitate the therapist intervening when the group threatens a defense that a member still needs, such as protecting a reticent member from premature probing. One infantile member, exhorted by the group to function as a man, spent a weekend in self-indulgent and destructive behavior.

2. Educate members from the very beginning that the group is a talking group only. The distinction between verbal communication and motor activity is maintained by appropriate reminders when the latter occurs ("what is John's foot saying?" "Could you put that look, or that fist, or that smile into words?" "What feeling is making you want to smoke, stand up, run out, or touch?"). Members are repeatedly educated to the idea that verbalizing feelings, thoughts, and memories is cooperative behavior, but acting on them in any way without prior discussion is uncooperative behavior.

3. Early in treatment, focus on dealing with obstacles (resistances) to the verbal expression of aggressive impulses. This significantly reduces the possibility that members will act on these impulses. This approach involves questions such as: "How do you all feel this group is going or not going?" "Do you think John is planning to return to this group next week?" "What could I or the group do to get each of you to walk out of here?" (Learning the conditions under which each would leave indicates the tolerance–intolerance level for certain feelings; the therapist is then in a better position to regulate the dosage for each member.) This

also involves willingness to establish the negative transference and not permit the positive transference to become too gratifying.

4. Accept responsibility for preserving the integrity of the group. The therapist thus gives priority to the resolution of treatment-destructive patterns of acting out.

5. Explore and analyze early subgroup formation: "Why are John and Mary more interested in each other than in anyone else in the group?" "Why is Mary telling her dream only to John?" "George, how do you think Ed feels toward Helen?" "Bob, how would you like to go to bed with Helen?"

STATUS QUO RESISTANCE

Status quo, inertia, or doldrum resistance usually appears after the first six months, when the members' presenting problems have been somewhat alleviated. This resistance reflects the feeling that maintenance of their present state of functioning is all that can be asked of them. This is demonstrated in wishes to drift along aimlessly and have a gratifying time together.

An adult group had been meeting for almost a year. The destructive resistances—lateness, absenteeism, monopolization, courting expulsion—had been resolved. Group members came regularly, expressed positive feelings for the group, and were understanding, supportive, and compassionate with one another. The group presented a picture of smoothly cohesive functioning. Sessions developed a uniform character.

Sue, a lonely divorcee, reported each week upon her success or failure in eliciting attention from men. She received weekly dosages of commiseration and encouragement to mingle, arrange parties, and go to dances.

Max regularly reported crises with his alcoholic wife. He consistently received support for his anger at her and tacit approval of his flirtations with other women.

Evelyn faithfully presented each new piece of outrageous behavior by her son-in-law and received specific advice on how to meet each new crisis.

Charlotte gave periodic resumés on her vague dissatisfactions with every significant life area, submitted the details of her psychosomatic ailments, and was met with bemused tolerance, advice, and teasing about her recurrent vaginal discharge.

Lyle entertained the group with his sardonic expressions of hatred for his mother and contempt for his ailing male lover.

A pleasant atmosphere enveloped the group. Forward movement had stopped. The members were quite content with the situation and were determined to maintain the even emotional tenor the group had achieved. The outstanding characteristic of this group's status quo resistance was the banishment of all negative feeling toward one another and the therapist. Competition, resentment, sexual jealousy, envy, the war of the sexes, the conflict of generations, and negative transference perceptions of one another were all swept under the rug.

The group's behavior supported the validity of the observation made by Ormont and Strean (1977): "There is a covert concurrence not to uncover anything that threatens the detente" (p. 121).

The critical steps toward the resolution of this resistance were taken when the therapist shared with the group his impression that, "We seem to have an unspoken agreement here to have only pleasant feelings for each other, and I wonder where all your other feelings are going." This intervention produced a flurry of complaint and derision against the therapist for seeking to disturb the group's placid atmosphere.

"What's with you? Can't you stand prosperity?"

"The poor guy is deprived—no one has been murdered in the group!"

"He's been going to Instigator School and he's just doing his homework."

"If you thought we were sitting on our feelings, where the hell were you before this?"

With the door opened by their spontaneous expression of negative feeling against the therapist, the members were able in ensuing sessions to release the feelings they had been suppressing toward one another. The women expressed their anger at Max for his subtle encouragement of his wife's drinking. The men confronted Sue with her consistent avoidance of emotional involvement with them which, in turn, elicited her fearful hostility toward males. Lyle's use of the group to gratify his sadistic wishes met sharp censure. The tolerance of Charlotte's vague complaints gave way to impatience with her too obvious reluctance to feel. Sessions became vibrant as the group increased its emotional repertoire to include the wide range of feeling between love and hate.

RESISTANCE TO ANALYTIC PROGRESS

This resistance represents fear of change and apprehension about moving ahead into unknown emotional areas. It is marked by considerably more anxiety than status quo resistance. A group in resistance to therapeutic progress may demonstrate long and uneasy silences, considerable uncertainty in what to discuss in the group, and insistent demands for direction and guidance from the therapist.

RESISTANCE TO TEAMWORK

This resistance features self-preoccupation, wishes for undivided attention, and unwillingness to listen to, learn from, or help others. Individuals utilizing this resistive pattern show little concern for other members and feel no responsibility for the welfare, healthy functioning, and integrity of the group. They can offer a variety of rationalizations for these uncooperative attitudes: "I can barely keep my own head above water.

Why should I help them?" "All my life I looked after myself, so I'll keep taking care of me and let them look after themselves."

At times the unwillingness to feel and assume any responsibility for the group is cloaked in attitudes of arrogance and contempt. One self-oriented member, a descendant of New England aristocracy, repeatedly derogated the group to her individual therapist as "that civil-service bunch," or as "that exercise in mediocrity."

A group in the throes of a resistance to teamwork will display indifference to the absences of its members and will ignore new members. Members will frequently interrupt one another to pursue their own pressing concerns, so the flow of the session is disrupted and the resolution and clearance of a given problem may be difficult.

This insularity and uncooperativeness may be expressed as a function of the negative transference to the therapist (or to the group as a whole). The individual, subgroup, or group engaging in resistance to teamwork is depriving the therapist of a cooperative and mutually helpful group—in effect, depriving the parent of a happy and harmoniously productive family. In dealing with this resistance, it is indicated that the therapist should clearly convey he is not interested in getting the group to work together but in *understanding* why they are unable to do so. This approach, combined with timely investigation of their wishes to deny him the satisfactions of competent group leadership, will generally elicit the feelings and memories being enacted in each member's support of the resistance. Intense conflict and competition with siblings, deep resentments associated with having been assigned responsibility for younger siblings, adolescent reprisals against demanding and controlling parents, and self-destructive refusal to grow up (the child's ultimate revenge against destructive parenting) all emerge as major themes in the process of resolving this resistance. (See Ormont and Strean 1978, Chapter 6.)

RESISTANCE TO TERMINATION

The fifth level in the sequential system of priorities is reached in termination resistance, which features a return to patterns of resistive behavior that had seemingly been outgrown but reappear during the final months of treatment (and on the eve of vacation breaks). In one group approaching termination, each member became involved in a crisis situation: a resurgence of perverse sexual obsession, a sudden eruption of marital conflict, a family upheaval over a son's wish to marry out of his religion, an abrupt job resignation, and a sudden decision to have a child. The therapist's observation, "From the look of things, it is obviously time to *start* this group rather than end it," drew smiles from the members. The crises abated as members were able to express their fears of being on their own, rather than seeking to convince the therapist, through their crisis-inducing behavior, that they were not ready. We are reminded of the aptness of the statement by Glover (1926) that at the approaching end of treatment, the patient, "apprehending loss of the transference situation endeavors to fall ill once more" (p. 45).

One group member, Charlotte, had made considerable gains in the group and had been talking about her growing readiness to leave. However, she was experiencing strong anxiety about giving up the group therapist, who had also been her individual analyst at one time and had seen her through various major crises. In a group discussion of Charlotte's conflict about terminating, another member told her, "Your only problem now is that you're addicted to Dr. B."

Several sessions later, Charlotte reported a vignette recounted to her by a friend who was an accomplished runner. The friend had been jogging slowly with her husband. After a mile or so, she had told him, "It's been nice talking to you, and now I'm going off to do some running on my own." Charlotte indicated that she had found this story very gratifying.

Seizing the cue, the therapist asked the group why Charlotte couldn't leave him behind and do some living on her own. Fortified by the therapist's willingness to permit her to separate and the confidence of the group in her capacity to function autonomously, Charlotte was able to resolve the feelings of attachment, loyalty, and dependency blocking her appropriate departure.

Another member, Rachel, had devoted a good part of her youth to the care of her widowed father and younger siblings. Although she had made significant therapeutic gains in recognizing and meeting her own emotional needs, she kept delaying termination on the basis of wanting to see one or another group member through some pressing life situation. Several members voiced their suspicions that it was Rachel's interest in the therapist that was keeping her in the group.

The therapist joined her resistance by saying that it sounded extremely selfish of Rachel to think of leaving when he needed her with him to help cure all present and future group members. Rachel's empathic rejoinder was, "To hell with you! I'm not falling for that line anymore." This response indicated that treatment had sufficiently immunized her against the longings for her father that she had gratified in the past by enacting the role of his wife and mother of his children. The group helped Rachel work through the residual components of her transference ties to them and the therapist, and she left several months later.

CHAPTER 6

The Resolution of Group Resistance

The profound significance for the patient of the resolution of resistance in individual psychoanalytic therapy was emphasized by Freud (1915–1917) in the *Introductory Lectures on Psychoanalysis,* where he stated that "the patient's mental life is permanently changed by overcoming these resistances, is lifted to a higher level of development and remains proof against fresh possibilities of illness" (p. 377).

Resistance resolution is of no less significance in group psychotherapy; it brings the group and its members to a higher level of functioning. A silent group whose resistance to verbalizing feelings is resolved, is raised from a preverbal, infantile level to that of verbal functioning. This constitutes a significant developmental ascent. A group tolerating a sadistic attack by one member upon another is involved in perversity. Asking such a group why its members are being party to such behavior invariably arouses anxiety in them. This anxiety arousal raises the level of group functioning from participation in sadomasochistic perversion to the higher level of neurotic functioning.

An example of group resistance offered earlier was that of an adolescent group that thirstily soaked up the details of one member's frantic sexual activity. The therapist's intervention— "How would you all like Jennie to excite you today?"—induced emotional discomfort in the group members. This changed the group atmosphere from one of unconflicted gratification of voyeurism-exhibitionism to awareness of their own participation in Jennie's sexual problem. From this came a group readiness to help Jennie talk about her feelings, rather than compulsively undress and exhibit herself in the group and outside relationships.

EXAMPLES OF GROUP RESISTANCE

The maturational effect of the resolution of a pervasive group resistance upon a group is illustrated in a report by Rosenthal (1971).

> A group of 16- to 18-year-old boys and girls spent the first several months of group treatment in repetitive complaints against the inadequacies and insensitive behavior of their parents, offering numerous illustrations of parental neglect of their emotional needs. Aware that denial of inadequacy or damage and projection onto parental figures were the group's fundamental defenses, the therapist helped group members maintain them. From time to time he acceptingly agreed (reflected) that their only major problem was dealing with their childlike parents, upon whom they could not depend.
>
> This theme was then followed by a sequence of sessions dominated by members' excited descriptions of indulgence in dangerous behavior. The boys described risking their lives by racing trains to railroad intersections and taking dangerous combinations of drugs. The girls demonstrated a marked lack of self-protectiveness in their reported sexual encounters with total strangers. An air of excitement pervaded the group.

At this point, the therapist explained to the group that because their parents had not taken proper protective care of them, they had never learned to properly protect themselves. The group members became quite thoughtful and serious. They expressed gratitude at the therapist's understanding, expressed wishes to live with the therapist as a family, and then each proceeded to soberly examine his own and one another's need to flirt with danger. A parentifying process developed by which the group, as a good parent, began to limit the self-destructive tendencies of its individual members. The boys expressed concern for the girls, conveying that they were entitled to resist sexual exploitation and make worthier object choices. The girls encouraged the boys to redirect their energies from dangerous childish pursuits to education and job preparation.

One group was consistently dominated by Helen, who session after session monopolized with her emotional accounts of her tension-laden relationships with husband, children and co-workers. Attempts by the therapist to deal with her resistance individually by exploring her need to dominate the sessions brought only temporary lulls in her flow of talk and achieved only cursory expressions of interest on her part in the problems and feelings of her fellow members. It was only when the therapist began a session by confronting the group resistance that the process of its resolution was set in motion. This was achieved when the therapist opened a session by asking "what would you all like Helen to talk about for the whole session today?"

This intervention interpreted the group's stake in Helen's resistance and their consequent need to uphold it. The members were then released to express their own anxieties around revealing their problems and inadequacies and their willingness to hide safely behind Helen's monopolization, even though at times they found themselves resenting her selfishness. As one member put it, "We resented her and used her at the same time." Another member with deep passivity problems added, "We could always count on Helen to get things going." A third member linked Helen with her own more aggressive sister who had dominated the stage in her own family and described that she had found a certain gratification in silently feeling contempt for Helen in her "piggish" behavior in the group. The therapist's engagement of this group resistance led to a more equitable sharing of time as other members began to examine Helen's hunger for attention and to point out to her that the group was set up for the benefit of all the members.

Monopolization operated as a resistance in another group in which two members, Sam and Claudia, utilized about 80 percent of the group's time.. Other members seemed generally tolerant of the subgroup monopoly. The eventual resolution of this resistance was set in motion by the therapist contacting the most silent group member, Dave. The fact that Dave had fallen asleep in the previous session had alerted the therapist to his need for attention, as well as providing a cue that it was time to deal with the group resistance.

The session began with one of the quieter members complaining that she had been interrupted in the previous session (by another nonmonopolizer). She added that one should not have to work so hard to be heard. The therapist then asked Dave whether he would be willing to help Sam and Claudia (the monopolizers) become more vocal in this group. Dave laughed and said they certainly didn't need any help from anyone.

Ray then said it seemed as if Dave needed help talking and asked why he was so quiet. Dave explained his silence as a protection against being hurt—"It's something I've learned from bitter experience." He then told the group of having been sent away to boarding school at the age of 14 because he criticized and opposed his parents' attempts to impose their intellectual interests upon him at the cost of his strong athletic involvement. Continuing to talk, Dave shared his painful social isolation at the school, his parents' constant favoritism of his sister, and his pervasive sense of exclusion from his family.

Group members' empathic responses to Dave removed the emotional barriers he had erected and enabled him to express a constellation of sad, hurt, and angry feelings. Dave's emergence into the group stimulated its interest in having him and the other less active members express themselves in each session. Over a period of several months, group talking time was utilized in an increasingly democratic manner, until a consistent pattern of fairly shared time was established.

In another illustration of the effect of resolving a group resistance, the rallying point for the resistance was the refusal of one member to pay for two sessions he missed because of a combined business and vacation trip.

When the therapist brought to the group's attention the fact that Sam's check did not cover the missed sessions, Sam quickly expressed his dissatisfaction with the accustomed procedure of members being responsible for all sessions, referring to it as "kind of cheap." The other members were initially silent spectators to what appeared to be a one-man rebellion. However, as Sam moved from protest to an impassioned tirade against the therapist for being "selfish, acquisitive, mercenary and money-grubbing," smiles and affirming nods from the onlookers gave evidence that a powerful group transference resistance was in the making.

Rachel made an applauding motion, and Alan offered encouragingly, "Good going, Sam—give it to him." Ted said admiringly that Sam was a "really gutsy guy," and Helen observed approvingly that Sam "really came alive." Bob joined the chorus of support for Sam's defiance by expressing his admiration for Sam: "He certainly doesn't-pull any punches, does he?"

Sam, obviously gratified at the show of support, responded with, "Why should I?" and then added defiantly, "He can stand on his head for the money!"

Aware that the resistance was at its height, the therapist chose this moment to tell the group that they were all out to defeat him and that Sam's rejection of the contract seemed to have special meaning for each of them.

Alan grinned and explained, "I always root for the underdog. When you're the runt of the litter like I was, you always get a kick out of someone telling off your smug big brother."

Bob offered this explanation of his stake in upholding the resistance: "When Sam first began to complain I thought he was being petty, but then I felt a sudden wave of anger at Dr. R. and I remembered how my father reneged on his promise to buy me a car when I got into college."

In bitter tones, Ted addressed Bob: "At least your father didn't break into your piggy bank! Can you imagine a grown man robbing his own kid! He never gave me a reason and he never paid me back, and I guess I never forgave him."

Rachel said, "I was getting quite a kick out of Sam's belligerence, and then I began to wonder if Dr. R. would punish him—maybe kick him out of the group."

Sam interjected sarcastically, "Thanks for your good wishes, Rachel."

Rachel continued, "That's right Sam—I think I was out to do you dirt. I used to egg on my little brother to do mischievous things, and then when he was in trouble with my parents, I'd feel more secure."

Viola, noncommittal until this point, sadly volunteered a childhood memory of using her meager allowance to buy flowers for a friend's birthday party. Upon arriving in bitter weather at the friend's home, she discovered that the party had been postponed. She had not been informed because her impoverished family did not have a phone. Viola described her vain attempt to return the flowers to the florist and her pervasive feeling of being cheated in the situation.

The members examined one another's patterns as enacted earlier in the sessions: Alan's need to hide behind the aggression of others toward authority; Rachel's need to instigate deviant behavior; Ted's vindictiveness; the anger and rebuke in Viola's patterned self-presentation as mistreated and cheated. The group then turned its attention to the now silently glum Sam with Alan observing that, "Sam looks disappointed because the revolution didn't come off." This signaled an investigation not only of the feelings which had prompted his outburst, but of those which underlay his constantly competitive attitude toward the therapist and operated disadvantageously is his frequent altercations with superiors on his job.

It is through the vehicle of resistance that the patient conveys his incapacity to engage consistently in spontaneous verbal communication. Thus, a contributant to the deep therapeutic significance of the resolution of a group resistance lies in the fact that it establishes a climate in which individual members can work on their own and one another's resistances to spontaneous emotional communication.

Prior to the dissolution of a groupwide resistance, the members perceive the resistance as ego-syntonic. With resolution, the contribution of each individual member to the shared resistance is rendered both dystonic and comprehensible. They begin to examine, with less defensiveness, their own and one another's behavior in upholding the resistance. The members are also then free to look at the character attitudes and defenses (Helen's garrulousness and Sam's competitive defiance) they have built up to deal with anxiety. The group-oriented approach to resistance apparently harnesses the group's inherent forces for the therapeutic benefit of all members. The management of a powerful group resistance of suppression of feeling is described here:

An adult group in a psychiatric outpatient setting was

characterized by an almost total inability of its members to directly express negative feeling of any kind toward one another, the group therapist, or the significant figures in their lives. Feelings of resentment and anger were enacted in lateness, absence, withholding silence, and vague threats to leave, or were avoided by group discussion of safe topics. Group sessions were dominated by Freda, a 60-year-old help-rejecting depressive who complained constantly about every aspect of her life and parried any potentially remedial suggestion that group members offered. At any hint of impatience with her monopolization or with the feelings of impotence she engendered in others, she would tearfully accuse them of not being interested in her. Attempts by the therapist to suggest that the members might be harboring negative feelings toward Freda were countered with blanket denial. In a session when Freda was absent, members justified her taking the lion's share of the time on the basis that "she needs it more." When Freda made a suicide attempt and was hospitalized, the group reacted with guilt, continuous concern about her, and continuing suppression of their negative feelings toward Freda, the therapist, and one another.

At this point the therapist sought supervision. He was helped to recognize that a massive group (ego) resistance was operative and that the key to its resolution lay in the group members feeling entitled to their anger against him. The therapist then designed his interventions to deal with the group's suppressed negative affect toward him. When the members wondered whether Freda would be helped in the hospital, the therapist raised questions about his own competence in having put Freda in the group in the first place, then having permitted her to monopolize their time, and then not having anticipated and forestalled her breakdown. Although the members disclaimed harboring these thoughts and assured the therapist that he had done his best, a palpable livening of the group atmosphere ensued.

In the next session, the therapist addressed the group's denial and contained feelings toward Freda by asking if he was the only one who was relieved by her departure. Again, there was no direct response to this, but later in the session, the members began the long-delayed process of identifying and reacting to one another's resistive patterns. Frank, a pedantic intellectual, had given the members a word test in the waitingroom, and this led to the group examining for the first time his need to present himself as the most informed and the most knowledgeable. When the members were describing how they felt like students being judged and graded by Frank, the therapist conveyed that his ego could withstand criticism by asking how his own performance in the group should be graded.

The next session featured the first direct criticism of the therapist when he was accused of showing more interest in a new member than he had shown in the senior members. At the following session, there was continued concern for Freda, as members asked about her condition and the disposition of her case. Abe then revealed a deep anxiety about his prostate condition. Another member expressed anxiety around traveling that had preoccupied her for a year but which she had not shared with the group because of its apparent disinterest.

The members tended to blame themselves for not speaking up. Here the therapist intervened to explain that if anyone was to blame, it was him for not setting a climate in which they *could* talk. Several members then complained that other members did not show interest when problems are raised. One expressed envy of another's improvement, and the latter expressed anger at the group for not recognizing her improvement. The envious member also noted his own response of withholding feeling when angry.

Barbara responded to the theme of suppressed feeling, indicating that she had been angry for months at the discussion of current events in the group. Barbara added pointedly that if she were retired, like Myra (an older woman who had entered the group right after Freda's departure), she might have the time to read all the newspapers and know about current events. Dora joined in, in a sharply hostile tone, "That's right. We're here to talk about our problems and not the news."

Eli said that when he first entered the group, he couldn't trust the strangers in it. Julia said she, too, was afraid to talk and for months she sat puzzled because no one filled her in (a complaint against the therapist). Barbara then talked of leaving the group because she was doing better, but then acknowledged that problems still existed with her husband. She described feeling ashamed of telling the group about his poor treatment of her because they might wonder why she put up with him and might feel that if she were healthier, she'd get rid of him. Eli interjected that he felt guilty about coming to the group and saying the same thing over and over—complaining about his phobias and not doing anything about them.

In this session we see the emerging catalytic effects of the therapist's changed emotional stance: open expression of intra-group negative feeling and progressive communication in the form of members sharing new information about themselves.

A session later, indirect aggression against the therapist was expressed in complaints about negligent, exploitive, and greedy doctors who prescribe inadequately tested drugs and cooperate with self-serving drug manufacturers. Abe then revealed to the group his insomnia and his profound fear of the malfunctioning of a catheter installed after his intestinal surgery. The members were self-critical for not talking about and overcoming their problems. Again, the group therapist redirected the aggression onto himself: "You people are always blaming yourselves, but it's my failure in not having arranged for you to be able to talk about and overcome your problems." He then asked who in the group had the right to be most disappointed in him. The group members seemed surprised and did not respond verbally.

The following session witnessed a tentative but significant initial approach to the previously taboo area of sex. Abe, whose life history was marked by sexual suppression, talked animatedly of a blatantly scatological TV program. Other members reported being shocked by the program. An air of excitement pervaded the group, followed by a heavy silence. The therapist's comment that everyone was frightened by the excitement generated by the talk of the TV show was met with denial. However, his observations that they were not ready to talk about sex elicited ready agreement. Members reported that in their childhood experiences, sex was taboo and not to be discussed. Eli indicated he never talked with anyone about sex and recalled how awed he was, as a young man, when his friends bragged of their sexual exploits.

A session held a month later illustrated the progress made by the group in achieving a greater freedom in expressing aggression. The session also illustrated the continuing tendency of group members to maintain the depressive pattern of turning the anger back upon their own egos.

Eli spent almost a third of the session describing recent events in his family and his feeling responses to these. He expressed fury at his wife's growing independence in going to work and learning to drive; in the past she had been dependent upon him. He reported having broken a vase in his anger and expressed guilt over his act. Several other members then were self-critical about their own anger. The therapist commented that they had never felt entitled to feel anger at those close to them. Eli and Barbara then told of never having been able to feel anger at their parents. Eli said his wife was not the only one he was angry at, and wondered why his parents hadn't done something about his problem in his adolescence. Eli added, "And I'm angry at the doctor, too," explaining that he had tried in vain to reach him during the week.

Barbara expressed her anger at the previous therapist for leaving, "The doctors go on and we're stuck behind." Dora angrily complained that they had not yet gotten a replacement, as the departing therapist had promised (the group had previously had co-therapists). When the therapist asked where the group's anger about this had been, Betty said that she usually blames herself; Eli said he usually just shuts up in the group when angry.

At the next session, Barbara reported having been able to talk with her husband about some of her unhappy feelings in the marriage. The other members gave her a spontaneous round of applause. Several members continued to air their longstanding driving anxiety. Janet described her panic while driving when she feels a wish to smash herself up, an impulse she connected with her wish to have her parents feel sorry for her. Abe began to discuss varying behavioral approaches available for the treatent of phobias, but when other members indicated they were more interested in his feelings than in the facts he was reciting, he spoke of deep feelings of anxiety and shame around his catheter. Group members expressed their understanding of his feelings of being different and stigmatized. Members then began to recall how they feared speaking up in class as children and the pains they took to avoid painful exposure. Eli would feign illness on days he was scheduled to talk in class. Janet recalled her feelings of always being different. Other members described their own poor view of themselves as children and their assumption that others felt the same way about them.

A group resistance frequently encountered in the early stage of group psychotherapy is that of the group's total absorption with the therapist, seeing him as an all-powerful source of help and gratification (Bion's basic-assumption dependency). In this emotional constellation, each member is primarily interested in interacting with the therapist. He views fellow members as having little to contribute to him and sees them mainly as rivals for the leader's attention. Members seek the leader's advice and opinions on almost any subject, and each member addresses his or her concerns directly to the leader.

In addressing this resistance, the group can be asked why they are all so much more interested in him than in one another. They can be told that they are all more interested in receiving individual treatment than in getting to know one another as a group, and that they seem bent on turning the sessions into a series of lectures by the therapist, rather than a setting for productive group therapy. When the resistance stems from the early deprivation of each of the members, the therapist may join the resistance by actively talking and feeding them words. Eventually the group will mature beyond the stage of dependence upon the mother for feeding, and its members will develop an interest in one another.

One group of adolescent girls met in a classroom arranged for each member to have a period of individual contact with the group leader in the group sessions. Members moved geographically closer to the leader as each took her turn for individual feeding. It should be noted that a countertransference resistance was operative here: The therapist gratified her own need to feel close to each member, rather than having the members relate to one another.

Another group of adolescent girls in a girls' parochial school setting displayed the opposite resistance, repeatedly presenting themselves to the therapist as a group. Members spoke as "we" rather than in the first person and invariably referred to feelings or experiences shared by the whole group: "We all hate this teacher—what can we do about it?" "Our parents don't want us to be alone with boys." This group resistance effectively protected any one member from exposure and prevented the therapist from knowing them as individuals. In effect, the therapist was faced with a group-transference resistance based on the members' wishes to express their aggressive and sexual wishes collectively, so the mother could not blame them individually for harboring these unsanctioned impulses.

An adult group in a private practice setting displayed a protracted pattern of expressing their feelings via facial expressions rather than verbally. Members would look angry, unhappy, or sad but would not initiate talk of these feelings. This preverbal ego resistance was resolved over a period of time by the group therapist giving individual attention to each member, recognizing his or her non-verbal behavior, and identifying the feeling he was conveying: "Bill looks sad."

One member, when told by the therapist that he seemed far away (isolated), reported a dream that revealed a wish to be clutched at by his wife. This dream appeared to represent all the members' need to be held by the mother. When the therapist symbolically met this maturational need through attention to each member on the preverbal level, the group was then enabled to attain a verbal level of functioning. Bill, whose silent unhappiness was recognized, revealed his fear of talking in the group and exposing himself. Helen, whose critical expression was noted by the therapist, expressed criticism of the therapist for not running the group more efficiently. Orin, when his pained expression was noted, spoke of his feelings of defeat and frustration at being constantly found wanting by his wife.

A group that had met for three and a half years was transferred when the group therapist relocated to another state. The replacement group therapist sought diligently to elicit the members' feelings around the abandonment. However, they denied having continuing feelings about the former group leader and did not reveal the content of their continuing individual phone contacts with him. The new therapist felt excluded by the barrier of the group's unvoiced absorption with and loyalty to the original therapist.

A strategy of joining the resistance was then adopted, in which the therapist repeatedly referred to her predecessor and acted as if he were, in a sense, still leading the group. In the midst of group interaction she would ask, "How would Dr. H. handle this?" or "What would Dr. H. say about this?" When a new member arrived, she introduced the members with, "This is Dr. H.'s old group." The members laughed and assured her that they were her group. She also suggested setting up a conference call to include Dr. H. in all group sessions and recommended that they maintain and even increase the frequency of their individual phone contacts with Dr. H., so they could continue to be helped by him. Group members giggled, chuckled, and smiled in response to these interventions.

As the therapist continued with this approach, feelings of sadness, longing, and resentment at the loss of Dr. H. emerged. Memories of being caught up in divided loyalties to their parents also surfaced. The member who had most represented the group's tie to Dr. H. finally told the current group therapist, with exasperation, "Look, let's cut out this crap! You're here now and Dr. H. isn't. Now we have to deal with you and with each other, so let's get down to business."

In a group of 13- to 15-year-old girls there was a lot of talk of sex, of wanting to defy their parents not only by having sex, but by having it with inappropriate males. One member, Yvonne, excitedly told of sex play with the handyman at her school. Amid this ongoing discussion of their sexual impulses, another member brought in a friend without discussing it with the therapist or the group. The visitor continued to come, with no comment about her presence made by anyone. The group was seen as defying the mother (the female therapist) by having an illegitimate child in the person of the visitor. Addressing Yvonne as one of the major spokesmen for the resistance, the therapist suggested that she could get a beautiful baby from the handyman. Shortly after, Yvonne voiced her fears of becoming pregnant. Another member warned her, "You'd better watch your step." A session or two later, the visitor quietly dropped out.

A senior citizens' group composed mostly of widows and widowers displayed a resistance of supporting its members in their reluctance to reveal and understand their feelings. One member, Fred, invariably had a tight, tense expression on his face. When the therapist tried to investigate this look, other members quickly attributed it to Fred's medication. There was a collective need to maintain emotional ignorance of their own and one another's feelings. The feelings being held in check by this resistance appeared to be anger at their deceased spouses and their sexual feelings, which they felt were not permissible at their age.

This resistance was steadily eroded under the impact of the therapist's continued bestowal of permission for anger and sexuality. When a male and female member whispered in a subgroup, the therapist observed that they seemed to get along well together and asked if they had thought of going to bed together. This was greeted with feigned shock and nervous laughter. The therapist also frequently suggested that they were entitled to anger at her intrusive questions and shocking statements. The resolution of this resistance was heralded several months later, when Fred requested that the therapist renew the medication for his chronic chest pains. Another member stated, "You don't need medication, Fred. All you have to do is talk here."

Another group was dominated for many sessions by the implacable hatred of two members for each other. Each threatened to leave because of the other. Each maintained that it was hopeless to talk to the other—"Whatever I say, she'll hate me." Finally each withdrew into hateful silence. The bitter impasse between the two members filled the sessions with tension and left the therapist feeling hopeless and in despair. This subgroup resistance was being upheld by a group resistance, since all the unvoiced aggression of the other members was being channeled into the subgroup. The subgroup was enacting anger for all the other members.

The resolution of this resistance began with the therapist asking, "What would happen if *everyone* expressed their angry feelings here? Who would each of you be most worried about?" This resulted in other group members expressing their negative feelings toward one another to some degree, but primarily toward the therapist. Considerable anxiety was also expressed about the possibility of counterattack from the therapist.

With this clearance of aggression, the group no longer needed to channel it into the subgroup, and the subgroup resistance was permanently resolved.

Mark and Cheryl, the two youngest members in an adult therapy group, were quite attracted to each other. When Mark mentioned wanting to sell his hi-fi set, Cheryl quickly expressed interest in buying it. Negotiations continued for several sessions and arrangements were made to meet outside the group, so Cheryl could inspect the item. The group's bemused tolerance of this behavior suggested a group resistance of gratification in the subgroup's acting in and planned acting-out behavior.

This resistance was addressed by the therapist asking the group, "Is there *anything else* you would all like to see Mark and Cheryl do together?" Several members giggled; several others were indignant. One responded to the intervention by suggesting the therapist get immediate help with *his* sexual problem. Over the next several sessions, members got in touch with their unvoiced feelings that had been upholding the resistance: primal-scene memories, memories of parental seductiveness, or parental prohibition of any hint of sexuality.

Group resistance presents the group therapist with his severest challenge. The encounter with the commonly shared feeling constellations in the group—especially that of mobilized aggression—can exert a heavy influence on the therapist's feelings of hatred, impotence, despair, anxiety, or confusion. Sleepiness and fatigue are common responses to sustained group resistance. The therapist who can tolerate these feelings and use them in the service of resolving group resistance has a powerful therapeutic tool at his disposal.

OVERCOMING VERSUS RESOLVING RESISTANCE

The initial stage of psychoanalysis was characterized by attempts to pressure and coerce a patient into surrendering his resistance to free association. In *Studies on Hysteria*, Breuer and Freud (1893–1895) noted that patients do not keep their promise to say everything that occurs to them. Referring to his practice of placing manual pressure on a patient's forehead to facilitate the recovery of memories, Freud states: "The only advantage gained is the fact that we have learned from the results of this method in which direction to investigate, and what things we have to force upon the patient. For some cases this suffices, for it is essentially a question of finding the secret and telling it to the patient so that he is more usually forced to relinquish the resistance" (p. 211).

The difference between forcibly overcoming and resolving resistance is a crucial one. In the resolution of resistance, patients are not subjected to undue pressure to give up their resistive behavior (with the exception of behavior that is destructive to the group or the treatment of any of its members). They are permitted to outgrow the need for the resistance and to give it up voluntarily. Overcoming the resistance frequently involves elements of criticism, pressure, and coercion in relation to a particular manifestation of resistance.

> Stewart, a biologist, entered a group of patients with psychosomatic disorders and quickly began to dominate it with authoritative discourses on the pros and cons of the

various drugs used by the members in the physical treatment of their illnesses. Stewart's briefcase held a store of pharmacologic research studies that he readily quoted from to buttress his opinions and also dispersed to the members.

As the group atmosphere increasingly assumed the character of a classroom, with Stewart as the teacher, the therapist became increasingly threatened and resentful. Her attempts to blunt Stewart's influence by suggesting to him that group members were entitled to differing opinions and that he might be squelching them were received with scant recognition. The members expressed their respect for Stewart's expert knowledge and their appreciation for his sharing this valuable information with them. A group resistance was clearly operating.

Changing her tack of vainly seeking to control Stewart or have the group limit him, the therapist joined the resistance. She praised his contribution of important knowledge to the group's fund of information and suggested that he prepare a series of formal presentations on the various drug therapies. The group reacted enthusiastically to the invitation and Stewart agreed, but added cautiously that it might take some time to prepare his talks. The therapist suggested a date in the near future and reminded Stewart of this at each session. A week before the first scheduled presentation, the therapist reminded him again and pointed out that everyone was looking forward to it.

Stewart, whose lecturing had diminished significantly since the therapist's initial invitation, expressed doubt that he could have his talk ready and suggested delaying it until some unspecified time in the future. The therapist expressed concern that the group would be disappointed.

At this point, various group members entered the discussion. One suggested letting Stewart "off the hook," since it appeared to be a burden. Another observed with humor that Stewart had already given enough information to last a lifetime. A third expressed that she thought she had enough facts and wanted to get back to the sharing of feeling that had characterized the group prior to Stewart's entry. As the members went on to examine why they had encouraged Stewart, it became clear that he had provided a welcome detour from the growing awareness of their angry feelings toward the significant figures in their lives.

In another illustration of breaking through resistance, a beginning group therapist was faced by a silent group in one of the early meetings. He told the group, "If you people want to get help, it's important that you talk." When the silence persisted, the therapist turned to the most dependent member and asked an information question about a reality problem the member had previously discussed. The member provided the information requested, other group members became involved, and the resistance was seemingly overcome. However, the therapist's pressuring tactics prevented him from gaining access to the apparently strong and significant feelings aroused by the beginning group psychotherapeutic experience, which were being held in check by the group resistance of silence.

A group of mothers in a children's psychiatric clinic increasingly frustrated their therapist by defensive avoidance of seeing their own contributions to their children's emotional problems. Determined to overcome their tenacious resistance and fueled by his own intense countertransference feelings, the therapist abruptly arranged for each member to undergo psychological testing. In his zeal to eliminate the resistance, he was unaware that he had forced his group members to psychologically disrobe before they were ready. Not surprisingly, the relationship between group and therapist never became a cooperative one.

Attempts at eliminating resistance by coercion or enforced surrender are neither helpful nor desirable. Discovery and translation of the emotional message contained in and concealed by the resistant behavior are the keys to resolution. Abolition of the resistance rarely achieves this end. It is in the application of the principles of resistance resolution that the therapist can most effectively aid his group in the task of surmounting the obstacles to emotional maturity. This is achieved by recognition of the resistances, by study of their historical and contemporary significance in the lives of group members, by deciding upon which resistance warrants priority attention, and by bringing to the group's attention the existence of the resistances to be approached. The group is then helped to verbally discharge accumulated instinctual energies, so the necessity for its maintaining a pathological resistance is diminished.

CHAPTER 7

Selection and Screening

At a time of widespread use of group psychotherapy, those involved in its teaching and supervision are aware of a continuing lack of understanding of the group's therapeutic potential and limitations. Patients who could do much better in a group languish in stalemated individual treatment. Others struggle to keep themselves afloat in a group setting where they are beyond their developmental depth (Freedman and Sweet 1954, Slavson 1955).

A prime candidate for group therapy is the patient who does not feel entitled to his/her own aggression and/or sexuality. The presence and example of other members, who are freer in the expression of these major feeling constellations, can have an activating and freeing impact upon those who restrict and suppress their aggressive and libidinal impulses.

One new group member witnessed an angry exchange between the group therapist and another member who, with strong affect, called the therapist "a damn liar!" The therapist retorted emphatically, "It's about time you found

out what a liar I can be." The member muttered, "At least
you admit it." The new member exclaimed in wonder,
"I've been in analysis for seven years, and I have never
spoken to my analyst like that." A third member commented, "Well, perhaps it's about time you did."

Mrs. W. was strongly defended against her negative
feelings toward her parents. In the intake interview at the
child-guidance clinic, when asked what her parents were
like, she could only respond concretely that her father was
a tailor and her mother a housewife. In view of her
emotional constriction, she was referred to a group. In one
of Mrs. W.'s early sessions, another member, Mrs. S.,
complained bitterly about her own mother and concluded
her indictment with a vehement, "I hate her!" Sessions
later, Mrs. W. reported that this incident had affected her
profoundly. She had been shocked to hear such a naked
expression of anger and, along with considerable anxiety,
felt as if a great weight had been lifted from her.

There are individuals who are emotionally illiterate in their
blatant ignorance of the language of feeling. They cannot or
dare not feel angry, jealous, rebellious, hurt, insulted, annoyed, peeved, sad, affectionate, loving, or joyous, nor do they
recognize these feelings in others. They do feel threatened and
inadequate when attempts are made to directly elicit these
feelings from them. In group psychotherapy, these constricted
personalities can remain in relative comfort on the emotional
periphery of the group and benefit from vicarious catharsis and
derivative insight until they are ready to participate more
directly. In individual therapy the same constriction, lack of
spontaneity, and continuous use of denial frequently results in
therapeutic impasse and mutual frustration for patient and
therapist. Groups activate, stimulate, and catalyze; they offer
ongoing exposure to the emotional facts of life without the
necessity for direct focus on egos and the invasive or toxic
effects of such contact.

There are others who, for varied reasons, cannot assimilate
the undiluted confines of the one-to-one treatment setting.

Some have been rendered too guarded and suspicious by pathological primary relationships. For these, the group setting's diluted relation to the parent–authority figure effects a much safer therapeutic environment. One woman, who remained strongly ill at ease and unspontaneous with her individual therapist, reacted with immediate interest when a group was casually broached to her. Asked why she felt so positively about a group, she responded, "I guess because groups have chaperones." She then revealed a previously withheld history of childhood sexual molestation.

Another category of patient for whom group therapy is indicated embraces those with pressing needs to engage in conflict with authority. Such individuals frequently devote their energies to defeating the "parent"-therapist. In the group setting, they encounter the palatable authority of their peers, who can exert much more therapeutic leverage on them than the therapist.

Characterologically ingrained patterns, when exposed to the emotional flux and fluidity of the group situation, are loosened and rendered accessible. In the group substitute family, the adaptational patterns the individual developed in his first family are repeatedly enacted and reenacted, perceived, recognized, and resonated to by fellow members. Aggressiveness, submissiveness, withdrawal, domination, diffidence, compliance, instigation, seduction, and provocation are repeated, lived out, held up to the mirror of the group, and impinged upon. Through the *emotional* learning inherent in these encounters, new patterns of adaptation and feeling are forged.

In evaluating a patient's suitability for group therapy, several determining factors are weighed. These relate primarily to the individual's nuclear problem, his experience in his primary relations, and the basic ego strengths established in these crucial early interactions. Referral to a group involves certain realities: the presence of sibling substitutes, with whom the therapist and time must be shared; direct exposure to the needs, impulses, and feelings of other patients; the ever-present possibility of encountering hostility from other patients. One woman, who was placed in a group while in the midst of a severe marital crisis, attended two sessions in which she functioned primarily as a highly sympathetic listener. She then called the therapist to announce her decision to withdraw from the group, tearfully explaining, "I just can't take it—their stories and problems just rip me apart. I think about them all week and then I have no energy left to deal with my own life— it's too much for me!"

A driven executive had expressed interest in group treatment because it was less expensive than individual therapy. However, in the consultation interview with the group therapist he signaled his unreadiness for a group by noting his intense frustration at coming up subway stairs and having the people ahead of him prevent him from bounding up three steps at a time. When asked how he might feel about listening to the problems and life stories of seven or eight others in a group, he conceded, "I just don't have the patience for that kind of thing—I'm just not built that way."

Unlike the individual therapist, the group therapist is unable to exert full control over the degree and kind of emotional stimulation to which any one member will be exposed. The group setting can thus never offer the same degree of protection and security attained in individual treatment.

These conditions suggest that certain minimal ego strengths and superego development are requisite to the capacity to assimilate a group psychotherapeutic experience. The individual should have attained some satisfaction in his first group-of-two with the mother, which would have developed some desire for object relations and group acceptance. When minimal gratifications on the earliest levels have been lacking in an individual's life history, a group placement may be equivalent to demanding that a 1- or 2-year-old adjust to nursery school. Spotnitz has noted that problems rooted in the preverbal period in the life of the individual patient are more effectively dealt with in the individual setting, since the group tends to inhibit the recall and presentation of those deeply *personal* problems of the oral and anal type.

The principle that group psychotherapy cannot be universally applied is illustrated in the following vignettes.

In the third meeting of the group, Ray began talking the moment his fellow members assembled. His words flowing swiftly, Ray described the hurt, resentful, and suspicious feelings aroused in him by a variety of interactions during the week with colleagues, superiors, friends, his girlfriend, and her parents. He likened each current situation to a similar experience in childhood, painting a detailed picture of lifelong deprivation, hurt, and resentment.

The other group members, who had been listening, alert and involved with Ray's presentation, began to succumb to the verbal inundation. Several moved restlessly in their seats, one yawned repeatedly, another stared at the ceiling, several sent appealing looks to the therapist, and one shrugged in apparent hopelessness. Ray, completely unaware of the overt behavior of the others, continued unabated, his words directed to no one in particular and his whole being involved in producing and hearing his own speech.

After almost one half hour of uninterrupted monologue, the group therapist intervened by asking, "How do you think the group is responding to you right now, Ray?" Ray reacted as if he had been shocked into wakefulness from a pleasant dream. He threw the therapist a murderous look, cast a fleeting glance of disinterest at his fellow members, complained that he was far from finished, and withdrew into a depressed, sullen silence.

Ray was obviously not emotionally old enough to share time and the therapist with a group. Like a hungry infant, he could only suck up all of the available "food" in the group. In a subsequent individual session he recalled stealing food from the plates of his siblings throughout his childhood.

The following vignette illustrates the destructive impact on a group of a member unable to control sadistic impulses.

Sylvia opened the session with the resentful statement that she wasn't understood by anyone in her fight with Don in the previous meeting. She expressed disappointment in Rita for never supporting her in fights with "the men" and told Jim that she had "only contempt" for him because of his neutral stand in the conflict. Without looking at Don, she said her stomach had turned when she saw him in the waiting room, adding that she had been hoping he'd left the group. When Don sought to discuss his feelings about the last session's conflict, Sylvia said venomously, "You're not worth talking to here." Then turning to Rita, she inquired, "How is your dog?"

Myra, the newest member, shared her feelings around her strained relationship with her husband. With obvious gratification, Sylvia urged Myra to leave her husband and, with gusto, offered suggestions such as, "Throw the food in his face," "Tell him to get the hell out and never come back except to babysit when you're with your lover." Myra, initially amused with Sylvia's responses, then tried to explain that she was not interested in war but in bettering the relationship. At this, Sylvia bristled and said with sarcasm, "Well, excuse me!" She then proceeded to ignore Myra.

When the therapist emphatically brought to her attention that she was acting on her feelings and that was not appropriate behavior, Sylvia retorted accusingly, "Why are you always picking on me? What about the big baby [Don]—why don't you ever tell him to behave?"

Sylvia is obviously too primitive to abide by the requirements of group psychotherapy. Her craving for excitement in aggression and her need to immediately gratify her sadistic impulses would keep any group in a constant state of tension and would pose a serious threat to the egos of her targets.

Horner (1975) wrote a significant paper on the unsuitability of such narcissistic personality disorders (as delineated by Kohut) for group treatment: "A critical aspect of this disorder is the incapacity to experience others as people in their own right.

It is assumed that their needs, feelings and motivations are the same as those of the self, and failure to keep in perfect harmony is experienced as an assault" (p. 302). Horner says that for these individuals, others exist only to gratify and to validate them. When others fail to meet these entitlement expectations, their reaction is that of the enraged infant whose bottle has been abruptly withdrawn. Horner observes that the outcome for such patients in group therapy, in her experience, "has been nonproductive for the patient at best and destructive for both patient and group at worst" (p. 304).

The deviant in the group may frequently be a valuable catalyst and spokesman for the repressed feelings of the more controlled and conforming members. However, groups have only a finite tolerance for difference, and the therapist must make a judgment as to the degree of deviancy that a given group can tolerate without treatment-destructive effects upon the group or the deviant. Shea (1954) noted that "there are definite limitations to this method [group]. It is contraindicated in patients with too limited a capacity to function with other human beings, in patients with problems too specialized for group identification or in patients with character makeups too brittle to permit relatively indelicate handling" (p. 257).

Group therapy as a preliminary form of therapeutic conditioning has been found helpful for children whose previous relations with significant adults have been so negative that they are unable to relate to an adult within the emotionally close quarters of the one-to-one setting. The group, with its diluted relationship to the therapist, supports their contemporary needs for emotional distance and can function as an antechamber to subsequent individual treatment.

Group therapy may also serve to wean a patient from an extended period of individual treatment, and as a testing and/or integration of treatment gains.

There is increasing use of concurrent individual and group treatment in private psychiatric and psychoanalytic practice. Individual therapists have reported that the addition of group therapy frequently activates and enriches the patient's individual therapeutic motivation and production. Fried (1955) has noted that "the benefits of combined therapy are due to the cross-fertilization between individual and group treatment. Each form of treatment enables the patient to take better advantage of the other form of treatment" (p. 194). Emphasizing the efficacy of this approach with passive–narcissistic patients, Fried points out: "The group makes the observation that behind a façade of cooperation and charm the narcissistic patient hides the fact that he has little or no true interest in others" (p. 199). Group censure, Fried observes, helps in resolving the serious technical problem that the treatment of these patients presents, namely that they experience their narcissism as ego-syntonic. "Through group pressure, narcissism is eroded into something that is ego-alien, and anxiety associated with a higher level of development is mobilized" (p. 200). The individual sessions in turn enable the patient to assimilate and withstand the anxiety activated in the group.

THE SCREENING INTERVIEW

Some group therapists draw their group members from their individual patients and thus are familiar with their major resistances, defenses, and ego resources prior to their entry into group therapy. Other therapists may have had no contact with an individual referred to them and must use a screening interview or interviews, as well as information available from the referral source (if any), to evaluate potential group members. These interviews are used to obtain information upon which to base a determination as to suitability for group therapy.

Two criteria are involved: How will the group affect the individual, and how will the individual affect the group? The therapist will seek predictive clues to the major resistances a future group member will utilize, and he will be especially alert to any indicators of treatment-destructive patterns, such as a history of leaving relationships, jobs, engagements, or marriages. In this initial encounter, a process of mutual appraisal occurs. The group therapist examines the candidate on various levels that have as their common denominator an effort to predict what role the patient may play in the group—what assets and deficits he may bring to the group, and how these will fit into the group culture. On the basis of his own dynamics and needs in the group situation, the therapist will also seek to assess and predict how the patient will feel and behave toward him in the group situation. Will he make the therapist feel comfortable or uncomfortable? Will he be ally, opponent, competitor, or neutral? The group therapist may inquire about the individual's problems and his ideas of how the group may help him. The therapist will also seek to determine if there are preconceived ideas of how the group will work, the expected duration of the group experience, and what the individual expects of the group therapist.

The candidate is concurrently making his own assessment and evaluation of the group therapist. He's seeking primarily to determine if the therapist is interested in him, if he is wanted by the therapist, and, most crucially, if the therapist will be a good parent to him in the presence of the group (family). Thus, he also assays the therapist's feelings, role, attitude, and behavior toward him in the group situation.

The prospective group member may express his anxiety, feelings of inadequacy, and unconscious testing of the group therapist by such statements as: "I'm not very good in groups. I don't talk much. It's not easy for me to speak up, so I don't know if the group is such a good idea for me."

An appropriate response to such a declaration of inability to give to the group might be, "It has been our experience that many people who are quiet or do not say much in groups have gotten just as much out of the group, if not more, than those who are always talking." With this response, the group therapist transforms the proffered inadequacy into an asset, saying, in effect, "I do not feel bound to accept or to agree with your self-devaluation, and I want you in spite of it."

Conversely, a group candidate may present himself as superior to the group. One father, to whom membership in a guidance group was broached, explained that he had already had considerable group experience in the P.T.A. and as an official in the Boy Scouts. The group leader replied, "In that case you should be very helpful to the group." The father beamed and promptly asked when the group would be meeting. In this situation, the group therapist showed himself not to be threatened by the candidate's competitiveness and interested in working with him (wanting him) despite it.

At times, a candidate may display marked indecision and ambivalence around the idea of entering a group. He may present almost equally balanced degrees of interest and avoidance, citing both potentially negative and positive features of the group experience. The group therapist may be tempted to respond to one of the ambivalent poles either by assuring the client that the group is worth trying or by suggesting that it might be better to forget it for a while. An alternative response to this blatant indecisiveness is for the therapist to simply reflect that there seem to be good reasons both for and against the group experience. A frequent response by candidates to such a reflection of their ambivalent feelings is, "Well, I guess I really can't say what will happen until I get in it and actually see for myself."

There are individuals whose life histories have produced feelings of worthlessness that cause them to see themselves as undeserving of any consideration, respect, or acceptance. When met with complete acceptance, they experience strong discomfort and suspect that any giving or considerate person will change his attitude toward them as soon as he finds out what they are really like. Such a person may resist acceptance into a group on the basis that he does not deem himself worthy of participating with others.

A comment by the group therapist to the effect that, "I don't know how the group experience will work out for you, Mr. X., because I don't know whether you'll be helpful to the group or find the group helpful to you," can be useful in overcoming this particular resistance. Implied in the group therapist's statement is that Mr. X. has an obligation to be helpful to others (guilt-relieving). It also raises the possibility that Mr. X., despite his damaged self-concept, may be of value to others (mildly ego strengthening). Concurrently, the statement enables Mr. X., if he so wishes, to maintain the fantasy that the group will expel him when it discovers what he is really like.

Some individuals enact self-defeating patterns that are traceable to their need for vengeful aggression against their parents. The child's most potent weapon against the parent lies in not growing up to be a healthy human being; he thus assaults his own ego in order to counterattack his parents. Such attitudes are frequently transferred to and enacted with subsequent authority figures who serve as parental surrogates, such as teachers, employers, therapists.

In treatment, the aim and effect of this powerful resistive constellation is to deprive the therapist of any satisfaction, to defeat his efforts to bring about positive change in the client's functioning and personality. Efforts at handling and eventually overcoming this resistance can begin in the screening interview when the group therapist indicates that the candidate may have either an unsuccessful or successful experience in the group but that in either case, the group therapist, for his own learning experience, will be interested in understanding why such an outcome resulted.

This approach serves to inform the defeat-authority-by-defeating-yourself person that the group therapist's ego is not dependent upon the candidate's success or failure. The therapist views both prospects with equanimity and, in fact, stands to gain in either case (by learning the reason for the result). The patient encounters a strong parental figure who will not be defeated by manipulation, and the healthy components of his ego can then be mobilized in the presence of the therapist, who seems capable of dealing with self-defeating patterns of long standing.

Clients are at times referred for group therapy and come to the screening interview preceded by the warmest recommendations and most positive affirmations for a group experience. In the face of this "advance publicity," a group therapist may be tempted to view the screening as little more than an informal tête-à-tête with the client prior to the latter's assured entry into the group. The following may illustrate the need for alertness on the part of the group therapist to such underlying factors as the client's feelings about his proposed group experience, the terms of the referral itself, and the referring person.

Mrs. P. was referred by her daughter's therapist who, from time to time, had seen Mrs. P. herself. The therapist suggested that a group might be helpful, and Mrs. P. quickly agreed. In the screening interview, Mrs. P., from the outset, exhibited a markedly pervasive need to present the wishes and thoughts of the authority—the referring therapist—rather than her own. When asked about her own ideas about the group, she stated that the therapist had recommended the group and "after all, she's a professional and you're one—so you both know what I need." She presented the assumption that if she were told that a group would be helpful to her, it inevitably must be so.

The group therapist, however, persisted in pointing out that he needed Mrs. P.'s help in evaluating whether or not she would be helpful to a group, or a group helpful to her. She again presented that she had no ideas of her own about this but was certain of the value of the professional recommendation that she enter a group. Although she still completely subordinated her own feelings, the group therapist began to detect a glow of gratification at his refusal to accept the submergence of Mrs. P.'s own ego.

Then, very timidly, she began to express some of her concerns that a group might not be for her, that she was fearful of a group, and that she probably would not be able to express herself as well as in the individual treatment situation. Then, apparently gathering more courage, Mrs. P. commented that her daughter had had a group and did not accomplish anything at all, but in individual treatment with the referring worker, was "doing beautifully."

The group therapist then commented, "Perhaps, like daughter, like mother." Mrs. P. glowed, laughed spontaneously for the first time in the interview, and then said in a heartfelt manner, "There are *many* things alike between mothers and daughters." She was then enabled to express more freely that she would "love" to be in individual treatment with her daughter's therapist. She was encouraged further to state that, even if she could not have this particular therapist individually, individual treatment with another therapist would be preferable to entering the group. The therapist then agreed that it seemed preferable for Mrs. P. to have individual treatment. She expressed gratitude that he had helped her to express her own wishes in this area.

Occasionally, a person is referred to group therapy on the basis of his individual therapist's negative countertransference feelings. Not infrequently the patient has induced feelings of helplessness, impotence, frustration, and rage in the therapist. These feelings may be acted on via a punitive expulsion of the patient from his "home" in individual treatment.

The patient usually senses the underlying motivation of the therapist, and his hurt and anger in the situation may often block a successful group adjustment. Alertness is indicated on the part of the group therapist to the nature of the referral and to the feelings of both the referral source and the candidate about the suggestion for group treatment. In the following vignette, an unresolved situation between the referring therapist and the candidate operated to influence the latter to present herself in the screening in a manner designed to ensure her rejection.

Mrs. A. had called to request an appointment to discuss entering a group. She began the session by staring belligerently at the therapist and saying, "I hope you're not one of those passive ones." Within the next twenty minutes, Mrs. A. angered the therapist by her anti-Semitic remarks, her question as to whether the therapist's group was smart enough for her, and her general attitude of contempt.

The therapist was fully aware of his wish never to see Mrs. A. again, much less invite her into his group, but he did not understand the source of her provocative behavior. He therefore commented that each of them felt uncertain that the group would be helpful to her or her helpful to the group, and asked whether she would be interested in another session to discuss it further. Mrs. A. was agreeable to this.

Mrs. A. began the next session by apologizing for her behavior at the previous meeting and recognized that she had been very unpleasant. The therapist said he had had the impression she was trying hard to get him to reject her, and he wondered why. Mrs. A. said she didn't know, but then recalled that she had initially wanted to go into group therapy with Dr. L. He had interviewed her, and Mrs. A. felt they had clicked. However, he did not have a group that met at a time she could attend. Dr. L. then referred her to the second group therapist, but added as she left the session, "If things don't work out with Dr. R., give me a call in September." Thus, Mrs. A. had been acting on Dr. L.'s underlying invitation to return to him rather than trying to reach an agreement with another group therapist.

The psychological validity of an individual's objections to participating in a group should not be minimized, for they are frequently rooted in early familial (group) experiences. Ormont (1957) has eloquently expressed this: "To ask a patient to venture into a group is often tantamount to asking him to return to his original family constellation with all its accompanying trauma, terror and personal tragedy; each objection is the scar tissue over an old wound" (p. 844). If the individual appears unready for a group experience, the group therapist may refer him back to individual treatment for further exploration of the anxieties and resistances involved. If the individual is not in treatment, the group therapist may hold a series of exploratory interviews, which may reveal the emotional core of the person's objections. In one person, a group may evoke memories of being exposed as inadequate and damaged in the family constellation; to another, it may portend a recapitulation of being emotionally burdened with the care of siblings.

The fruitfulness of exploring the feelings underlying the

stated request for group therapy is illustrated in the next two screening vignettes.

> Mrs. B., a 38-year-old school counselor, presented herself as cooperative, responsive, and knowledgeable about groups. She described the anticipated advantages of a group in providing "feedback" about the impact of her personality on others and how they perceived her emotionally. However, just beneath the surface of her intelligent amiability was a discernible layer of sadness and tension. This prompted the therapist to say that although she had given an accurate picture of what transpires in group therapy, he wondered what her feelings were about entering a group. Mrs. B.'s eyes flooded, and she said with deep hurt, "Well, my husband says I need to get into a group to get the hell kicked out of me." The therapist in turn asked, "Then why are you so cooperative with your husband's destructive wishes toward you?" Mrs. B. wept and was then able to express her own interest in individual treatment to deal with her lifelong pattern of submerging her own wishes and needs to those of others. Two years later, after achieving significant gains in individual analysis, Mrs. B. eagerly joined a group in combination with the continuing individual treatment.

In the following screening interview, the patient's expressed interest in a group operated in the service of his pathology.

> Mr. P., a 35-year-old attorney, presented the major complaint of overall absence of gratification in his life. He felt that participation in a group would stimulate his dulled emotions, basing this opinion on his past experience in encounter groups, which he had found "exciting and exhilarating." When asked about his current life situation, Mr. P. said he was married with two children, one an infant. He sadly reported the termination of an intense affair when the woman recently left the country. He did

not volunteer any information about his marriage, but when asked, indicated there was little communication with his wife. He added, with little apparent concern, that she was quite depressed and could barely care for the baby.

When asked if he were contemplating another affair, Mr. P.'s somber mood swiftly changed, and he spoke excitedly of a young woman in his office with whom he was conducting a developing flirtation. At several points in the session, he reiterated that the encounter group experiences had exhilarated him and given him "a high." At the close of the interview, the therapist suggested to Mr. P. that although a group would probably be quite exciting, it might be more to his advantage to work out his serious family problems in individual therapy. In effect, the therapist indicated that Mr. P. needed help more than he needed excitement. His craving for excitement (in affairs and in groups) enabled him to avoid feeling and dealing with his underlying depression and with the crisis in his family.

The screening session may be used to obtain predictive cues and valuable prescriptions for resolving the resistances the patient will enact in the group.

In her screening interview, Mrs. B. spoke admiringly of the friend who had referred her. Describing the friend as a wonderfully patient nursery school teacher, Mrs. B. reported how this friend had tolerated the aggression— even being spat upon—of a disturbed child for a whole year without even punishing him or sending him away from school. After this, Mrs. B. reported, this child had become a model student. The therapist took this as Mrs. B.'s communication of her own unconscious need to sorely tempt the therapist to expel her from the group. Forewarned and forearmed with this understanding, the group therapist was able to withstand Mrs. B.'s provocative attacks in the first year of her group treatment. She subsequently became a cooperative group member.

Mr. M. had had a considerable amount of individual analysis with several therapists. He presented a strong interest in joining a group, based upon a wish to experience the genuine emotional reactions of peers. Toward the close of the screening interview, he was asked how the group therapist might be of help to him in the group. Mr. M. seemed surprised and said he hadn't really thought much about that. He guessed that it was the therapist's job to provide the group and to keep it going.

The group therapist understood this response as a prescription for the amount of emotional contact Mr. M. wanted from him in the group—in this case, very little. Accordingly, when Mr. M. joined the group the therapist refrained from any investigation, exploration, clarification, confrontation, or interpretation with him. Mr. M. was allowed to interact with the group, and the therapist rarely addressed him, except to occasionally elicit his impression of another member.

After about three months, other members began to comment on the therapist's careful avoidance of direct contact with Mr. M. as compared with his freedom in interacting with and making contact with others. When another member asked Mr. M. what he thought of the situation, he gestured toward the therapist and said almost grudgingly, "He's not so dumb." Subsequently, Mr. M. told the group about his overwhelming father, who never permitted him any autonomy.

The processes of screening and selection of group members are obviously in close relation to the composition of particular groups. Since the group, and the interpersonal and interactive area it provides, is the instrument of treatment, its constitution, and especially its balance, require special attention.

Slavson (1955) has emphasized that " . . . a true psychotherapeutic group presupposes the planful choice of patients and grouping of them on the basis of clinical diagnosis and on the known or assumed effect they may have upon one another" (p. 4). Slavson (1955) has also stated, "One of the chief aims of grouping is to achieve a permissible quantum of pathology and hostility density" (p. 7).

A group composed solely of shy, withdrawn, and essentially uncommunicative individuals would offer meager opportunity for stimulation among its members and would impose severe burdens on the therapist and the group itself. Similarly, a group inhabited exclusively by volatile, highly aggressive personalities could produce a chaotic environment as therapeutically unsound as the emotionally arid climate in the group of withdrawn patients. It is the admixture of different personalities and behavior patterns, with ample representation of the major feeling polarities of love and aggression, which offers a psychological arena rich in interstimulation and cross-fertilization potential.

The presence of instigators—those individuals who can act as spokesmen for major feeling constellations such as aggression or sexuality—is a *sine qua non* for successful group psychotherapy. One such member was Mrs. K., a young widow who became the group spokesman for pregenital sexuality. She pleasurably reported incidents of men seeking to molest her on the subway. She described one friend who leaves the door wide open when using the toilet and another who goes out without underwear. She talked animatedly of the sexual misbehavior of married women in her neighborhood. Under the impact of feelings activated by Mrs. K., other more inhibited members recalled childhood sexual traumata and were helped to realize their sexual impulses toward their siblings, their children, and one another. Mrs. K. thus rendered a vital instigative service to the other members in heightening their emotional perception of their own sexuality; they, in turn, exerted a gradually maturing influence upon her.

Experience has shown that inclusion of certain carefully selected borderline schizophrenic individuals in groups has proven highly beneficial to them and to the groups. Nagelberg and Rosenthal (1955) suggested that a borderline child whose pathology does not cause him to be perceived as markedly different from his peers, and thus too threatening to them, may well be included in the group.

The collective group atmosphere created by the more normal individuals composing it would appear to exert a maturing influence upon the weaker ego structure of the borderline patient. In turn, he may contribute to the group by acting as an instigator in expressing for other group members their own, more deeply embedded anxieties around threatening situations and experiences in the [group] therapeutic settings. [p. 173]

This tolerance is specific to each group and its own unique configuration.

Group balance thus involves the presence of instigators who will stimulate the group without overloading its capacity to assimilate hostility and pathology. The combination of active and inactive, fearful and courageous, withdrawn and outgoing personalities is a vital factor in the creation of a feeling-laden, yet assimilable, current of interaction.

PREPARING THE GROUP FOR NEW MEMBERS

Related to the process of the selection and preparation of new members is the process of the preparation of the group for new members. Using the family as the basic paradigm, the addition of a new member is comparable to the arrival of a new baby in the family. As such, it is a group event of considerable consequence due to its evocation of past sibling trauma and rivalry in the lives of group members. The group therapist, as the parent surrogate, assumes responsibility for preparing the group for the newcomer and for helping the members express their feelings, anxieties, and fantasies about the coming event.

Reactions to the new member will depend largely upon the developmental level of the group and upon the life histories of its individual members. A group on the oral level will anticipate the new member as a rival for the available food and attention of the mother. One such group, when told by the therapist that there was someone interested in joining them, responded with the following plaintive comments.

"Gee, there's hardly enough time to talk as it is."

"I hope he's not a talker."

"This place is getting to be like Grand Central Station!"

"Since there will be less time for each of us, can't you lower the fee?"

A group on the anal level might react to the news of an expected addition with feelings of vindictiveness and threats of retaliation.

"Maybe it's time for me to leave—the new guy can have my seat."

"Don't expect to be paid on time from now on."

"You can bring somebody in, but we don't have to talk to them."

With a group on the oedipal level, reactions will cohere around feelings of sexual rivalry. The men may hope for an attractive woman; the women may anxiously ask the age of an expected female member, or they may, in turn, hope for an attractive male. Members of the opposite sex may react with feelings of sexual betrayal by the therapist. A group may seek to cajole, seduce, or pressure the therapist into rescinding his decision to add a member.

"We're all doing so well. Everybody is getting helped—we're really a good group now—why do you want to spoil it by changing the mix?"

"That's right. A good coach doesn't break up a winning combination."

"We'll all have to sit around now and waste precious time waiting for the new person to catch up."

At times, the group may seek to strike a bargain aimed at restricting the therapist's freedom of action with regard to new members: "All right, we'll accept this one, but will you promise that this is the last?

> One group spontaneously took a vote when the therapist announced a new member and then triumphantly confronted him with an obvious "majority against" decision. The therapist responded, "If this group were a workshop in democracy, I would have to abide by the majority opinion. However, since this is a therapy group based

upon psychoanalytic principles, I do not feel bound by the vote." This response permitted the group members to therapeutically express their anger.

"This is a damn dictatorship!"

"He always has to run the show."

"It's a waste of time to talk to that phony—he pretends interest in our opinion and then does whatever he wants."

When the therapist facilitates the expression of all feelings about new members and at the same time remains firmly in charge of the procedure for adding to the group family, he is fulfilling his therapeutic responsibility. Neglecting to inform a group of the arrival of a new member may result in excessive additional hostility toward the newcomer and may represent countertransference resistance on the part of the therapist. Some therapists seek to reduce the initial anxiety of the new member by bringing in two new members at the same time. Experience has shown, however, that two new members do not necessarily relate to or support each other. In addition, a group encounters more difficulty in accommodating "twins" than it does a "single birth."

CHAPTER 8

Countertransference and Counterresistance

T he concept of countertransference was briefly presented by Freud (1910) who described it as "a result of the patient's influence on the analyst's unconscious feelings" (p. 149). Freud insisted this phenomenon should be recognized and overcome by the analyst. The discovery of countertransference and its significance in therapeutic work gave rise to the institution of didactic analysis, which became the basis of psychoanalytic training. Yet, countertransference received scant attention over the next forty years, with the notable exception of Fenichel (1941) who stated frankly, "Whether the analyst should be angered by resistances of his patients or should welcome them seems to be a ridiculous question. Whoever is blocked in any piece of work to which he is devoted becomes annoyed" (p. 580).

Winnicott (1949) offered a useful differentiation of two major sources of countertransference: The "truly objective countertransference . . . the analyst's love and hate in reaction to the actual personality and behavior of the patient, based on objective observation" (p. 70). These realistically induced feelings are to be distinguished from the reactions attributable to the therapist's own insufficiently analyzed reaction patterns–the subjective countertransference.

The silence on the subject lifted rather abruptly in the 1950s, when countertransference became a matter of frequent reference, examination, and varying interpretations.

Countertransference has been called the analyst's reaction to the patient's transference, the analyst's own transference reaction to the patient, and the total of the analyst's reaction to his patients, including rapport, human understanding, empathy, and dedication.

Little (1951) offered a definition embracing the analyst's total response to the patient's needs, differentiating between objective and subjective countertransference reactions.

Similarly, Annie Reich (1951) differentiated between "countertransference in the proper sense" and the "analyst's using the analysis for acting out purposes."

Heimann (1950) dealt with countertransference as a tool for understanding the patient. The "basic assumption is that the analyst's unconscious understands that of his patient. This rapport on the deep level comes to the surface in the form of feelings which the analyst notices in response to his patient, in his countertransference" (p. 81).

Maxwell Gitelson (1952), in a frequently quoted paper, distinguished between the analyst's reactions to the patient as a whole and his reactions to partial aspects of the patient. The first occur in the initial contacts with the patient and "derive their interfering quality from the fact that they emanate from a surviving neurotic *transference potential* in the analyst." If these persist so strongly that the analyst cannot resolve them, the progress in the preliminary stage of treatment is impeded, the analyst, says Gitelson, must conclude he is unsuitable for this particular patient and refer him elsewhere.

The second type of countertransference–reactions to partial aspects of the patient–appears later, within an established analytic situation, and is seen as comprising the analyst's reaction to: (1) the patient's transference; (2) the material the patient brings in; and (3) the reactions of the patient to the analyst as a person.

The countertransference is then defined by Gitelson (1952) as the "activation of unanalyzed and unintegrated aspects of the analyst, and in dealing with this the analyst makes use of a spontaneous state of continuing self-analysis." (p. 1).

Racker (1957) conceived of countertransference as an inevitable component of the treatment situation. "Every transference situation provokes a countertransference situation. These countertransferences may be repressed or emotionally blocked but probably they cannot be avoided; certainly they should not be avoided if full understanding is to be achieved. These countertransference reactions are governed by the laws of the general and individual unconscious" (p. 303). Racker stresses the factor of reciprocity in transference-countertransference. Thus, every positive transference situation is answered by a positive countertransference; every negative transference is met by a negative reaction from the analyst (p. 303).

Kernberg (1975) studied countertransference literature and noted two contrasting approaches: First, there is the classical approach, which defines its concept of countertransference as the unconscious reaction of the therapist to the patient's transference. Second, there is the totalistic approach, which views countertransference as the total emotional reaction of the therapist to the patient in the treatment situation. This school of thought believes that the therapist's conscious and unconscious reactions to the patient are reactions to the patient's reality as well as to his transference, and to the analyst's own reality needs as well as to his neurotic needs. This also implies that although countertransference should certainly be resolved, it is useful in gaining added understanding of the patient.

The term *counterresistance* offered by Glover (1928) refers to acts or behaviors, inimical to the treatment, provoked in the analyst by his countertransference.

COUNTERTRANSFERENCE AND COUNTERRESISTANCE IN GROUP PSYCHOTHERAPY

One of the earliest references to countertransference in group therapy was made by Slavson (1943): "Frequently the therapist's own reactions need to be discussed. His unconscious responses, frustrations and traumatic experiences are often activated through the behavior of some of the children. This behavior (similar to his own in childhood as to that of his siblings) may outrage his sense of justice or arouse compassion" (p. 31).

In his first group therapy paper, Spotnitz (1947) suggested that the complicated types of transference and countertransference that develop in the course of group therapy require further investigation. Then, Spotnitz and Gabriel (1950), in a paper on resistance in group therapy, described the "induced resistances" of the therapist: "It was inevitable that the attempts of the therapist to guide the group in the direction of emotional remembering would result in the induction in her of impulses responsive to the needs of the group which would also act as a resistance to the desired functioning of the group" (p. 78). The authors identified several of these induced resistances as the therapist's strong desire to correct the personal deficiencies of group members when they were emphasizing their inadequacies and desires to avoid subject matter that might result in hostility from the whole group. The position of the therapist was described as extremely difficult, since, "she was exposed to the emotions of individuals, multiplied and intensified by their numbers who aimed at bending her to their will" (p. 79).

Another early reference to counterresistance in group psychotherapy was made by Ezriel (1950), who discussed the possibility of the group therapist seducing group members into having individual sessions.

In an editorial in the first issue of the *International Journal of Group Psychotherapy* (1951), Loeser, then president of the American Group Psychotherapy Association, noted a tendency to avoid the subject of countertransference and the implied presence of a taboo in this area. Loeser stated, "While the same criticism may well be leveled at the literature on individual therapy, it is less excusable in group therapy studies. I have the impression that the present emphasis on techniques and practices represents, in some way, a tacit collective resistance toward examination of factors involving countertransference" (p. 5).

Spotnitz (1952) discussed the impact upon the group thera-pist of the common (group) resistances that "tend to stimulate in the group therapist counter-resistances and the common group neurosis tends to induce in him an induced neurosis" (p. 8). Spotnitz adds: "The problem of self-analysis and self-control for the group therapist is a much more difficult one than for the analyst treating individual patients. In order to help the group members deal with their group resistances, the therapist must become aware of much more powerful resistances within himself as they are generated by the group and he must be able to understand them correctly" (p. 8).

The growing interest in the subject of countertransference in the group psychotherapeutic setting was reflected in the Octo-ber 1953 issue of the *International Journal of Group Psychotherapy*, which was devoted to a symposium on the subject. One of the contributors, Martin Grotjahn, viewed the countertransference as a necessary and integral element in the therapeutic process and stated, "As the group progresses to a working unit, multiple transference relationships will be developed and the therapist will react with feelings of countertransference. He *needs this feeling* in order to establish contact and to understand by empathy his patient's transference" (Grotjahn 1953, p. 41). The therapist's ego must observe, evaluate, and interpret, while his feelings simultaneously respond to the network of multiple transference. Grotjahn declares, in the language of Glover, that the group situation almost forces the therapist to use, observe, and analyze his feelings of countertransference; that countertransference, "corresponding to group transfer-ence," has to be analyzed or resolved when it becomes a counterresistance, "corresponding to group resistance" (p. 412).

In discussing differences in countertransference in individ-ual and group psychotherapy, Grotjahn observes that the individual analyst sees the reflection of his countertransference in the mirror of his patient's associations, whereas group psychotherapy is like working in front of a gallery of mirrors that are curved to reflect countertransference feelings. It is also noted that the patient in individual analysis has scant defenses against the analyst's countertransference, but the group offers a considerable degree of protection to its members.

In one group that had lost two middle-aged women members within a six-month period, a younger woman member confronted the male therapist with, "Don't you think you should solve your problem with older women?" Groups will rise to the defense of a member they observe to be the victim of a therapist's negative countertransference, and they will bring to a therapist's attention, either directly or indirectly, his singling out a member for special interest or preference. One knowledgeable group member, who was the subject of repeated praise from the therapist, finally asked him point-blank, "Why are you trying to separate me from my peers?"

A group member's dream—of the therapist giving out candy to the group when the dreamer wanted bread—alerted the therapist to his basic countertransference problem with the group. In his wish for a happy group family and a pervasive atmosphere of sweetness and light, the therapist was avoiding the members' aggressive feelings toward himself and one another.

Another group took its therapist to task for his favoritism toward one of its members. They confronted him with his pattern of expressing appreciation and praise to the favorite, to a degree noticeably greater than that accorded any other member. Group members explained the consequences of this preferential treatment: It disturbed their relationships with both the therapist and the favored member.

Groups are also effective monitors of the negative countertransference resistances of their therapist. One was asked why he invariably interrupted any woman member who expressed a forthright opinion. Another therapist was told by a group spokesman, "You always seem disappointed in us. We can't seem to measure up to your vision of the ideal group."

A group of girls in latency had dwindled down to a membership of two. New members were available for the replenishment of the group, but the therapist seemed paralyzed by the objections of the remaining members to any new members. Although she recognized the need to rebuild the group, the therapist was immobilized by her unconscious identification with the feelings of the two girls. After weeks of discussion of the situation in supervision, the therapist recalled that in her own latency period, a cousin had abruptly been brought into her home to live. With the attainment of this insight, the therapist's subjective countertransference resistance to augmenting her group was resolved.

Another therapist mildly suggested to a new group that it might be better if members did not socialize together and then added, more emphatically, that if they did, it was necessary to discuss it in the group. In the next few months several incidents of socialization occurred, which were dutifully reported to the group. Then the tempo and intensity of the outside contacts among members accelerated, until it assumed group-threatening dimensions and the therapist confronted the group with its behavior. The members responded with their understanding that the therapist had not really been opposed to this behavior, but had been interested in it being brought into the group for discussion. The therapist was left to deal with his own unconscious voyeurism, with which the group had been so cooperative.

Loeser and Bry (1953) noted that groups are remarkably responsive to countertransference and "to the extent that countertransference is defensive in nature, the effect on the group is usually adverse" (p. 393). They suggested that the most common reactions influencing the behavior of therapists are those based on identification. When this occurs in an area where the therapist's own dynamic processes are in conflict, anxiety and tension occur and acting out may result. Other forms of countertransference reactions are observed: (1) passivity and permissiveness as a cloak for unconscious hostility; (2) feelings of omnipotence leading to the concept of the healing touch; (3) pedagogic attitudes (the feeling that to heal is to teach); (4) sexual interest in patients; and (5) narcissistic power motives.

Slavson (1953) identified therapists' needs to achieve positive results—"aim-attachment"—with individual members and with the group as a whole, as an important source of counter-transference. He recognized both the therapeutically poor impact of a group therapist's uncontrolled countertransference and the heavy emotional task imposed by confrontation with a group. He observed that blind spots in the therapist's uncon-scious and overreactions to group members, to the whole group, and especially to the productions of his patients, diminish the therapist's effectiveness and, in some instances, may even make him unfit for his task. "There are his needs to be effective, to succeed, to get results. There is the actual or threatened mobilization of hostility and negative transference toward him in the group as a whole with which he may or may not cope" (p. 374).

In an unusually frank and nondefensive paper, Goodman and colleagues (1964) drew on their experiences as group therapists, and as participants in a peer-group supervisory process, to make a basic point: "When the group therapist, recognizing that he is confronted with a group in a state of resistance, finds himself unable to analyze, reduce, or remove the resistance, it is most probable that his own countertrans-ference distortions are part and parcel of the resistance and the main deterrent to its successful handling" (p. 340). The authors present clinical material from their own practice depicting both subtle and obvious variables in the therapist that enhanced resistance in an individual group member and a group. Each illustration describes an unconscious response of the therapist to an attempt by a particular group member to place him in what he feels is an early and unresolved familial position or conflict. In describing their own peer-group experience, the authors indicate that, with struggle and practice, they were able to help one another recognize attempts to reenact and resolve their own family situations within their groups. "It became possible to observe that wherever passive or active therapist behavior proceeded from personal distortions, the impact on the group was one which had a boomerang effect on the therapist and a blocking effect on the group process" (p. 341). The authors conclude that "the evidence of failure of groups or members was connected to failures of the therapists to see the part they played in inducing or compounding the resistance within the group" (p. 341).

Objective countertransference was discussed by Spotnitz (1968):

> Constant exposure to the instinctual forces operating simultaneously in the group members generates strong feelings in the therapist. If these are conceptualized as countertransference, they should be differentiated from feeling responses related to his own adjustment patterns. The feelings that are induced by the members' transference emotions are *realistic* reactions to what is going on in the group. [p. 21]

Ormont (1970–1971) recommended the planful use of the objective countertransference as a potent tool in the resolution of group resistance: "The group analyst, if he is in emphatic resonance with the group's emotional vibrations, will experience powerful feelings quite as a matter of course. Such feelings are a natural product of the total group interaction. They are vital, if primitive, messages from the members' shared unconscious emotions" (p. 69).

> The leader of a group of fathers of autistic children felt an intense need to help them with their underlying feelings of hopelessness and despair. This need was translated into a dogged pressuring of group members to express their suppressed and repressed feelings toward their severely withdrawn children. Group members reacted with silence, withdrawal, lateness, and frequent absences. In a group therapy seminar, the therapist was helped to understand that he was operating on the feelings induced in him by his group members; he was reenacting with them the driven need they had to get their children to talk, respond, and achieve. At times the therapist was induced to act autistically himself: When a father was locked out of the building and was unable to get into the session, all the

therapist could say at the next session was, "I wonder who locked the door."

Just as resistance in the group setting is as varied as that seen in individual treatment settings, so counterresistance can assume many shapes and forms in the group therapist.

The members of one group enacted their needs for closeness with one another by repeatedly meeting outside the group. The group therapist, in the grip of his own unresolved need for closeness with his mother, was unable to curb the acting-out behavior.

Another group therapist was unable to limit the monopolizing behavior of an infantile member with whom he identified; both had grown up under conditions of severe deprivation in very large families.

A beginning group therapist enacted his own rebellion against his overcontrolling parents by refusing to give any directions to his group members as to how they should behave in group sessions. As a result, the group functioned in an aimless fashion with serious dilution of the group therapeutic process caused by considerable extragroup socialization.

In a group of five women and three men, the major group resistance was enacted in the efforts of the women to obtain some token of special interest from the male therapist. Some members sought this gratification by displaying sexual interest in the therapist, others by striving to present their problems as more severe than those of their rivals. This group resistance was upheld by the therapist's own counterresistance based on his need to be the object of the sexual feelings of the women members and also to be the preeminent source of emotional nurture in the group. In order to maintain this position, the therapist tended to dominate the group with constant activity. He began sessions by eliciting the feelings of the women members toward himself or by sharing his feelings towards them. He also sought to attain greater intimacy with individual members by referring to material and issues they had brought up in recent individual sessions. He engaged in sexual repartee with the women. An air of intense rivalry among the women pervaded the group; the men were neglected and resentful.

In supervision, the therapist was enabled to become aware of his need to make up for a loveless childhood by enacting a harem fantasy in the group. He was then able to study, rather than gratify, members' seductive overtures, to pay attention to the men, and to develop a group-oriented, member-to-member interactive process. As he was increasingly able to control his behavior, group members recognized the change and responded to it positively. They attributed the change to his awareness that they were now mature enough to work things out with one another.

The use of co-therapists adds another parameter for transference and countertransference.

One therapist, in a session from which her male co-therapist was absent, permitted the male members of their adolescent group to dismantle his tape recorder. By this laissez-faire attitude, she was enacting an id counterresistance in responding to the boys' thinly veiled wishes to eliminate the male leader and possess her. The male therapist, for his part, tended to focus on one attractive, seductive girl in the group, making deep interpretations of the dreams she presented directly to him.

In a couples' group marked by considerable hostility and competitiveness of spouses toward each other, the male and female co-therapists struggled for control of the group, and each aligned himself with the same sex subgroup. When the supervisor began a conference with the two by asking, "How is your civil war group?" emotional awareness of their countertransference resistance was begun. With insight into how they had been sucked into the vortex of the group struggle, and with recall of their

own sibling strife, the therapists were able to work cooperatively together, to the considerably therapeutic benefit
of the group.

An adolescent girls' group therapist happily shared intimate
details of her own adolescence. In supervision, she justified
this on the basis of the rewarding degree of closeness achieved
between herself and the group. Here we see another illustration of an id counterresistance derived from the unconscious
need for intimacy. This process of sharing her own life history
with the group came to a halt when the members began to
pressure the therapist for more and more details of her sexual
experiences.

The death of a group member prompted a therapist to
immediately phone all the other members, to inform them of
the event. The therapist's rationale for this intervention was
that the members had a right to know of this very significant
group event. Exploration in supervision of the emotional
impact of the death upon the therapist uncovered his compelling need to swiftly share this intolerable burden. Here, a
hidden gratification of relief was achieved in the guise of a
therapeutic intervention.

In a situation similar to the one above, a group member
received a telephone call during a session and then left, looking
quite pale. A short time later, the member called to explain that
her mother had just died. The therapist was quite shaken by
this and felt an intense need to convey support to this member.
She then announced to the group that she was planning to
attend the funeral and suggested the group do the same. The
therapist demonstrated a potent identification with the be-
reaved member, originating in her feelings around the death of
her own mother.

Members of a group of early adolescent, predelinquent girls
repeatedly ran out of the meeting room, crawled under the
table to look at the female therapist's legs, jostled one another,
and generally indulged their impulses for excitement and
defiance. The therapist controlled her mounting frustration
and anger. Her explanation and interpretations of their behav-

ior were designed to avoid dealing with the problems and the underlying desire induced in her by the group to tell them that they had been behaving like "a bunch of little bitches" rather than a therapy group, and that she was seriously considering throwing them out.

A participant in a group-therapy workshop repeatedly, with much anxiety, presented crisis situations involving Anne, one of his group members. Study of the anxious feelings induced in the group therapist—and in the other workshop members whenever Anne was discussed—led to the understanding that she had been repeatedly exposed as a very young child to sharp dosages of anxiety. Here the objective countertransference was employed to attain understanding of the member's life history.

MAJOR SOURCES OF COUNTERTRANSFERENCE RESISTANCE

Acts of countertransference resistance originate in several major subjective emotional constellations that therapists bring to their groups.

THE NEED FOR A HAPPY FAMILY

Expressions of intragroup hostility, tension, and disharmony are often a necessary prelude to a group's attainment of integrated and cooperative functioning. However, some therapists have a need for their groups to offer a serene familial setting dominated by positive feeling and mutual helpfulness. In these groups, a subtle suppression of feelings of resentment, rivalry, hostility, and anger may prevail. This may be achieved by avoidance deflection, mediation, humor, and exhortation.

In the seventh session of an adult group, the war of the sexes began to emerge in some initial skirmishes. When a woman member hotly charged a male member with being crudely insensitive, the therapist hurriedly pointed out to the accuser that she was displacing onto the group member the anger she felt toward her husband. This intervention, in effect, prevented the two members from working through the negative feelings between them, blocked the woman from attaining emotional insight into her relationship with her husband, and served notice on the group that anger was not welcome. Another therapist, confronted with a simmering situation between rivalrous members, deflectively addressed himself instead to a third member, inquiring about an event in her life outside the group.

THE NEED TO BE LIKED AND REACTIONS TO AGGRESSION AND HOSTILITY

Many therapists acknowledge the principle that group psychotherapy offers a setting in which all feelings can be expressed in language. However, when actually faced with their groups, some therapists prefer affection, admiration, warmth, and respect. When members' transference hatred emerges (as it inevitably must), these therapists feel wounded by accusations that they are not helpful or understanding or that they show preference for other siblings in the group family.

The therapist may become narcissistically preoccupied with his hurt feelings. He is then highly susceptible to acts of countertransference resistance, which may be enacted in any of the following: avoidance of the aggression, counterattack via hostile interpretation, attempts to enlist other members as allies in squelching or refuting the attacker, expelling the attacker, or covertly encouraging the attacker to leave.

One therapist, who habitually contacted absent members, forgot to call a criticizing member who missed two consecutive sessions. Another therapist, faced with an upsurge of complaints and some threats of termination, stated that no one should leave without discussing such a decision for one session. In effect he was approving of the acting out.

The wish to avoid hostility, especially that emanating from the whole group, may explain why a large number of group therapists prefer to deal separately with individual members, rather than facilitate the emergence of groupwide expressions of negative transference and resistance. The therapist who is not under pressure to be liked and appreciated is free to objectively explore why members feel they are not being helped. He is able to commend a critic for his honesty, and is capable of enjoying feelings of competence when group members are able to express the whole range of human feeling toward him.

REACTIONS TO COMPETITION AND OPPOSITION

Therapists' needs for the assertion of authority and control may seriously interfere with the attainment of the group's coherent potential for growth and maturation. Therapists may find it difficult to share responsibility with the group for the behavior of its members. In the face of uncooperative behavior by an individual or subgroup, they are unable to ask, "Why are you all permitting this?"

> Mrs. R., a member of a new group of mothers, had taken a very active role, asking questions of other members, offering advice and interpretations, and directing the flow of discussion. In a note to the supervisor, the therapist wrote, "I am most concerned with Mrs. R. and how to handle her. I feel helpless and inadequate to cope with her competitiveness with fellow members and particularly with me. I am in the middle of a power struggle with her—and I have to get out."
>
> At the next group session, Mrs. R. was the first to arrive and spoke of her developing interest in obtaining training in social work, in the hope of eventually becoming a practitioner. She asked the therapist what *her* training had been and what degrees were necessary. The therapist abruptly changed the subject by inquiring about Mrs. R.'s marital problem.
>
> The threatened therapist had thus communicated to Mrs. R., "I don't want to hear about your wishes to become as good as I am; I only want to hear about your problems (deficiencies)."
>
> Mrs. R.'s need to present herself as adequate in the

group was easily resolved by the therapist joining her in this desire. For several sessions, the therapist solicited Mrs. R.'s opinions on how to help other members and what direction the group discussion should take. Highly pleased, she responded with constructive suggestions for a while and then asked the therapist, "Why am I doing your job here? I have my own problems to work on."

A young therapist encountered a highly aggressive, bright, and perceptive new member, who demonstrated a need to swiftly answer any questions put to the therapist by fellow members. Unable to control his resentful feelings, the therapist sarcastically addressed her as Doctor. The combination of lack of experience and his own unresolved rivalry problems prevented the therapist from using his induced feelings to understand this patient's own rivalry-ridden childhood, and kept him from studying her need to compete and from allowing the group to deal with her behavior.

THERAPEUTIC ZEAL

One of the strongest sources of countertransference resistance resides in the therapist's compelling desire to have his patients improve, make progress, and achieve a cure. When acted upon, this brings about a situation in which the therapist is out to cure before the patient is ready to be more mature, responsible, competent, adult and gratified. Overt and covert demands upon patients for achievement and mature functioning, made without regard to their emotional age and current level of development, can have highly adverse therapeutic effects in inducing regression and the use of more pathological defenses. To one patient, the demand for achievement may signify premature ejection from the crib; another may experience the demand as a second edition of a precipitous toilet training. When patients seek to comply with therapists' and fellow group members' pressure for change and growth by attempting life tasks and separations that are beyond the reach of their available ego resources, serious regression may ensue.

One group, at the behest of its therapist, mobilized to help a member overcome a longstanding dependence upon heavy dosages of tranquilizing drugs. Whole sessions were devoted to the problem as Beth was exhorted by all to abstain. Any slight reduction in her drug intake was received with applause, praise, and further encouragement to continue the improvement. Members called Beth at home to monitor her progress. Initially, Beth basked in the unaccustomed attention and expressed feelings of profound gratitude to fellow members for their unselfish efforts on her behalf. The therapist, who had originally emphasized the seriousness of Beth's addiction to the group, was highly gratified by his group's display of devotion to one of its members.

However, as the group maintained its pressure on Beth to conquer her drug dependency, she became less communicative. She began to arrive late to sessions, showed signs of depression, and hinted at the presence of suicidal thoughts. In addition, several of the other members began to withdraw in sessions, and others began to complain of newly developing somatic symptoms. Disquieted by this turn of events, the therapist presented the group at a group-therapy seminar.

There it was agreed that a crisis situation had developed. Beth's drug dependency was a defense against an underlying psychotic process, and all pressure on Beth to improve—and on the group to help her improve—was to be immediately lifted.

At the following session, the therapist asked the group members and Beth how they felt about the recent focus on her. This exploration released considerable suppressed feeling. Group members described having felt cheated of their legitimate share of the group's time and attention and resentful that the therapist obviously saw Beth's problems as having higher priority. All acknowledged mounting hostility toward the therapist and Beth. Beth explained that after the first flush of gratification at the group's interest, she began to feel increasing desperation over meeting the group's expectations. At the same time, her anxiety about appearing ungrateful for the group's concern blocked her from expressing her feeling of being hounded.

IDENTIFICATION WITH GROUP MEMBERS

In this category of countertransference resistance, the therapist is unable to separate himself emotionally from the patient with whom he identifies. He is not free to use his own induced feelings and reactions to the patient, since they are the same as the patient's responses. If the member with whom the therapist identifies complains of not having been helped or understood, the therapist will assume the member is justified in his complaint, and this emotional agreement can effectively block the member's aggression toward the therapist.

Special forms of countertransference may be operative in the referral or nonreferral of patients to groups. Patients who are frustrating, defeating, attacking, nonproductive, or boring may be referred to groups on the basis of intense negative feelings induced in their therapists. Transfer of a patient to a group may, in some cases, be the equivalent of an unwanted troublesome child being sent away to boarding school. The timing of a patient's entry into a group may be influenced by either subjective or induced countertransference factors. One therapist, who in his own childhood was prematurely confronted with stringent demands for grownup behavior, enacted a pattern of putting patients into groups long before they were ready.

The counterpart of the countertransferential group referral is the countertransferential nonreferral. A variety of factors may be involved when therapists do not utilize group therapy for their patients. Among these are a lack of understanding of the therapeutic dynamics of the group; the therapist's own unresolved wishes to remain close to a parent; feelings and memories of painful group experiences routed in his own family group. Some therapists may view with anxiety the prospect of exposing their therapeutic endeavors to others by referring patients to groups.

Initially viewed in negative terms as an interfering factor to be eliminated, countertransference has now attained a much more positive aura; it is recognized not only as an inevitable component of treatment, but as a desirable one. With this more benign attitude prevailing, therapists no longer have to feel unentitled to their love and hate feelings towards their patients and can welcome and use them to attain greater understanding.

Resistance has been presented in many of the forms and shapes it assumes in the group setting. Resistances ranging from the harmless and benevolent to the menacingly group-destructive have been identified and illustrated on individual member, subgroup, and group-wide levels. These identified resistances have been accompanied by approaches and techniques for resolving them. Resistance is an inevitable and ubiquitous dimension of the treatment situation that serves as a vital, albeit primitive and indirect, communication of the patient's life history and patterns of adjustment to family life. It is in the resolution of these resistances that group members achieve higher levels of maturity. It is hoped that the reader will have gained a sharpened alertness to the principles involved in forming groups, to selection on the basis of the patient's emotional age and his capacities to withstand the stress of group membership, to the presence of overt and covert manifestations of resistance, and to the powerful currents of countertransference feeling that groups are so capable of arousing. In this framework the therapist can help to liberate a group of human beings from the tyranny of unconscious impulse patterns they do not comprehend.

References

Aronson, M. (1967). Resistance in individual and group psythotherapy. *American Journal of Psychotherapy* 21:87–94.

Becker, B., Gusrae, R., and Berger, E. (1956). Adolescent group psychotherapy: a community mental health program. *International Journal of Group Psychotherapy* 6:300–316.

Berger, M. (1962). The function of the leader in developing and maintaining a working psychotherapeutic group. In *International Handbook of Group Psychotherapy*, ed. J. Moreno, pp. 79–93. New York: New York Library.

Beukenkamp, C. (1955). The nature of orality as revealed in group psychotherapy. *International Journal of Group Psychotherapy* 5:339–345.

Bion, W. R. (1948–1951). *Experience in Groups and Other Papers*. New York: Basic Books, 1959.

Bowers, M., Berkowitz, B., and Brecher, S. (1958). Therapeutic implications of analytic group psychotherapy with religious personnel. *International Journal of Group Psychotherapy* 8:243–256.

Breuer, J., and Freud, S. (1893–1895). Studies on hysteria. *Standard Edition* 2:1–369.

Bross, R. (1966). The "deserter" in group therapy. *International Journal of Group Psychotherapy* 6:392–404.

Bry, T. (1951). Varieties of resistance in group psychotherapy. *International Journal of Group Psychotherapy* 1:106–114.

Burrow, T. (1927). The group method of analysis. *Psychoanalytic Review* 14:268–280.

Cameron, J., and Freeman, T. (1956). Group psychotherapy in affective disorders. *International Journal of Group Psychotherapy* 6:235–257.

Cameron, J., and Stewart, R. (1955). Observations on group psychotherapy with chronic psychoneurotic patients. *International Journal of Group Psychotherapy* 5:346–360.

Durkin, H. (1954). *Group Therapy for Mothers of Problem Children.* Springfield, IL: Charles C Thomas.

———— (1956). Group psychotherapy with mothers. In *The Fields of Group Psychotherapy,* ed. S. Slavson, pp. 153–169. New York: Schocken Books.

———— (1964). *The Group in Depth.* New York: International Universities Press.

Ezriel, H. (1950). A psychoanalytic approach to group treatment. *British Journal of Medical Psychology* 23:50–74.

———— (1952). Notes on psychoanalytic group therapy. *Psychiatry* 15:119–126.

Fenichel, O. (1941). Problems of psychoanalytic technique. *The Psychiatric Quarterly* 10:18–36.

———— (1945). *The Psychoanalytic Theory of Neurosis.* New York: W. W. Norton.

Foulkes, S. (1946). On group analysis. *International Journal of Psycho-Analysis* 27:46–51.

———— (1957). Group-analytic dynamics with special reference to psychoanalytic concepts. *International Journal of Group Psychotherapy* 5:40–58.

Frank, J. Ascher, W., Nash, H., Margolin, J., et al. (1952). Behavioral patterns in early meetings of therapeutic groups. *American Journal of Psychotherapy* 108:10–18.

Freedman, M., and Sweet, R. (1954). Some specific features of group psychotherapy and their implications for selection. *International Journal of Group Psychotherapy* 4:355–368.

Freud, A. (1936). *The Ego and the Mechanism of Defense.* New York: International Universities Press.

Freud, S. (1900). The interpretation of dreams. *Standard Edition* 4:1–310.

———— (1904). Freud's psycho-analytic method. *Standard Edition* 7:249–254.

———— (1905). Fragment of an analysis of a case of hysteria. *Standard Edition* 7:3–112.

———— (1910). Observations on wild analysis. *Standard Edition* 11:219–230.

———— (1912). The dynamics of transference. *Standard Edition* 12:97–108.

———— (1913). On beginning the treatment. *Standard Edition* 12:121–144.

———— (1914). Remembering, repeating and working through. *Standard Edition* 12:145–156.

———— (1915). Observations on transference love. *Standard Edition* 12:157–171.

———— (1915–1917). Introductory lectures on psychoanalysis. *Standard Edition* 15/16:15–463.

———— (1921). Group psychology and the analysis of the ego. *Standard Edition* 18:67–144.

———— (1926). Inhibitions, symptoms and anxiety. *Standard Edition* 20:87–175.

———— (1937). Analysis terminable and interminable. *Standard Edition* 23:209–254.

———— (1954). Letter to Fliess. In *Sigmund Freud's Letters: The Origin of Psychoanalysis,* ed. A. Freud, M. Bonaparte, and E. Kris, p. 226. New York: Basic Books.

Fried, E. (1955). Combined group and individual therapy with passive-narcissistic patients. *International Journal of Group Psychotherapy* 5:194–203.

Gadpaille, W. (1959). Observations on the sequence of resistances in groups of adolescent delinquents. *International Journal of Group Psychotherapy* 9:275–286.

Gitelson, M. (1952). The emotional position of the analyst in the psychoanalytic situation. *International Journal of Psycho-Analysis* 33:1–10.

Glatzer, H. (1952). Transference in group therapy. *American Journal of Orthopsychiatry*

22:499–509.

_____ (1953). Handling of transference resistance in group therapy. *Psychoanalytic Review* 40:36–43.

Glover, E. (1926). A technical form of resistance. *International Journal of Psycho-Analysis* 10:377–382.

_____ (1928). *The Technique of Psychoanalysis*. New York: International Universities Press, 1955.

Goodman, M., Marks, M., and Rockberger, H. (1964). Resistance in group psychotherapy enhanced by the countertransference reactions of the therapist. *International Journal of Group Psychotherapy* 14:332–343.

Greenson, R. (1967). *The Technique and Practice of Psychoanalysis*. New York: International Universities Press.

Grotjahn, M. (1953). Special aspects of countertransference in analytic group psychotherapy. *International Journal of Group Psychotherapy* 3:407–416.

Heimann, A. (1950). On countertransference. *International Journal of Psycho-Analysis* 31:81–84.

Horner, A. (1975). A characterological contraindication for group psychotherapy. *Journal of the American Academy of Psychoanalysis* 3:301–305.

Hulse, W. (1965). Curative elements in group psychotherapy. In *Topical Problems of Psychotherapy*, vol. 5, ed. A. Kadis and C. Winick, pp. 90–101. New York: S. Karger.

Jackson, J. (1962). The transference neurosis in group psychotherapy. *Journal of Psychoanalysis in Groups* 1:54–60.

Jackson, J., and Grotjahn, M. (1958). The treatment of oral defenses by combined individual and group psychotherapy. *International Journal of Group Psychotherapy* 8:373–382.

Johnson, J. (1963). *Group Therapy: A Practical Approach*. New York: McGraw-Hill.

Kadis, A., Krasner, J., Winick, C., and Foulkes, S. H. (1963). *A Practicum of Group Psychotherapy*. New York: Harper & Row.

Kernberg, O. (1975). *Borderline Conditions and Pathological Narcissism*. New York: Jason Aronson.

Kotkov, B. (1957a). Common forms of resistance in group psychotherapy. *Psychoanalytic Review* 44:86–96.

_____ (1957b). Sexual fantasies in group psychotherapy. *Psychoanalytic Review* 44:146–153.

Kubie, L. (1958). Some theoretical concepts underlying the relationship between individual and group psychotherapies. Discussion by S. Foulkes and M. Grotjahn. *International Journal of Group Psychotherapy* 8:1–44.

Lazell, E. (1921). The group treatment of dementia praecox. *Psychoanalytic Review* 8:168–179.

Leopold, H. (1959). The problem of working through in group psychotherapy. *International Journal of Group Psychotherapy* 9:287–293.

Little, M. (1951). Countertransference and the patient's response to it. *International Journal of Psycho-Analysis* 32:32–40.

Locke, N. (1966). Group psychotherapy, group psychoanalysis and scientific method. In *The International Handbook of Group Psychotherapy*, ed. J. Moreno, pp. 294–298. New York: Philosophical Library.

Loeser, L. (1951). Editorial. *International Journal of Group Psychotherapy* 1:3–6.

Loeser, L., and Bry, T. (1953). The position of the group therapist in transference and countertransference. *International Journal of Group Psychotherapy* 3:389–406.

Mally, M., and Ogston, W. (1964). Treatment of the "untreatables." *International Journal of Group Psychotherapy* 14:369–373.

Mann, J. (1951). An analytically oriented study of groups. *Journal of Psychiatric Social Work* 20:137–142.

_____ (1955). Some theoretic concepts of the group process. *International Journal of Group Psychotherapy* 5:235–241.

_____ (1962). Psychoanalytic observations regarding conformity in groups. *International Journal of Group Psychotherapy* 12:3–13.

Marsh, L. (1931). Group treatment of the psychoses by the psychological equivalent of the revival. *Mental Hygiene* 15:328–349.

McCormick, C. (1957). Group dynamics: homeopathic treatment. *International Journal of Group Psychotherapy* 1:103–112.

Menninger, W. (1958). *Theory of Psychoanalytic Technique.* New York: Basic Books.

Morse, P., Gessay, L., and Karpe, R. (1955). The effect of group therapy in reducing resistance to individual psychotherapy: a case study. *International Journal of Group Psychotherapy* 5:261–269.

Moses, M., and Schwartz, D. (1958). A crisis in a prison therapy group. *International Journal of Group Therapy* 8:445–458.

Nagelberg, L., and Rosenthal, L. (1955). Validation of selection of patients for activity group therapy. *International Journal of Group Psychotherapy* 5:380–391.

Ormont, L. (1957). The preparation of patients for group psychoanalysis. *American Journal of Psychotherapy* 11:841–854.

_____ (1964). The resolution of resistance by conjoint analysis. *Psychoanalytic Review* 51:426–437.

_____ (1968). Group resistance and the therapy contract. *International Journal of Group Psychotherapy* 18:147–154.

_____ (1969). Group resistance and the therapeutic contract. *International Journal of Group Psychotherapy* 19:420–432.

_____ (1970–1971). Use of the objective countertransference to resolve group resistance. *Group Process* 3:95–110.

_____ (1974). The treatment of preoedipal resistance in the group setting. *Psychoanalytic Review* 61:429–441.

_____ (1977). Presented at Heed University.

Ormont, L., and Strean, H. (1978). *The Practice of Conjoint Therapy.* New York: Human Sciences Press.

Parloff, M. (1968). Analytic group psychotherapy. In *Modern Psychoanalysis,* ed. J. Marmor, pp. 492–531. New York: Basic Books.

Powdermaker, F., and Frank, J. D. (1953). *Group Psychotherapy.* Cambridge, MA: Harvard University Press.

Prados, M. (1951). The use of films in psychotherapy. *American Journal of Orthopsychiatry* 21:36–43.

_____ (1953). Special technical aspects of group psychotherapy. *International Journal of Group Psychotherapy* 3:131–142.

Pratt, J. H. (1907). The class method in treating consumption in the homes of the poor. *Journal of the American Medical Association* 49:755–759.

Racker, H. (1957). The meaning and uses of countertransference. *Psychoanalytic Quarterly* 26:303–357.

Redl, F. (1948). Resistance in therapy groups. *Human Relations* 1:307–320.

Reich, A. (1951). On countertransference. *International Journal of Psycho-Analysis* 32:25–31.

Reich, W. (1928). On character analysis. In *The Psychoanalytic Reader*, ed. R. Fleiss, pp. 78–103. New York: International Universities Press, 1948.

_____ (1929). The genital character and the neurotic character. In *The Psychoanalytic Reader*, ed. R. Fleiss, pp. 104–126. New York: International Universities Press, 1948.

_____ (1933). *Character Analysis*. Trans. by T. Wolfe. New York: Orgone Institute Press, 1945.

Reik, T. (1924). Some remarks on the study of resistances. *International Journal of Psycho-Analysis* 5:141–154.

Rosenthal, D., Frank, J., and Nash, E. (1954). The self-righteous moralist in early meetings of therapeutic groups. *Psychiatry* 17:3–9.

Rosenthal, L. (1968). Some aspects of interpretation in group therapy. In *Use of Interpretation in Treatment*, ed. E. Hammer, pp. 339–343. New York: Grune & Stratton.

_____ (1971). Some dynamics of resistance and therapeutic management in adolescent group therapy. *Psychoanalytic Review* 58:354–366.

_____ (1976). The resolution of group-destructive resistance in modern group analysis. *Journal of Modern Psychoanalysis* 1:243–256.

_____ (1978). An investigation of the relationship between therapists' orientations and their preferences for interventions in group psychotherapy. Doctoral dissertation, New York University.

_____ (1979). The significance of the resolution of group resistance in group analysis. *Journal of Modern Psychoanalysis* 4:83–103.

_____ (1980). Resistance in group therapy: the interrelationship of individual and group resistance. In *Group and Family Therapy 1980*, ed. L. Wolberg and M. Aronson, pp. 79–93. New York: Brunner/Mazel.

_____ (1985). A modern analytic approach to group resistance. *Journal of Modern Psychoanalysis* 10:165–182.

Scheidlinger, S. (1964). Identification, the sense of belonging and of identity in small groups. *International Journal of Group Psychotherapy* 14:291–306.

Schilder, P. (1936). The analysis of ideologies as a psychotherapeutic method, especially in group treatment. *American Journal of Psychiatry* 93:601–617.

Schulman, I. (1957). Modifications in group therapy with antisocial adolescents. *International Journal of Group Psychotherapy* 7:310–317.

Shea, J. (1954). Differentials in resistance reactions in individual and group psychotherapy. *International Journal of Group Psychotherapy* 4:253–261.

Shellow, R., Ward, J., and Rubenfeld, M. (1958). Group therapy and the institutionalized delinquent. *International Journal of Group Psychotherapy* 8:265–275.

Slavson, S. (1943). *An Introduction to Group Therapy*. New York: Commonwealth Fund.

_____ (1950). *Analytic Group Psychotherapy*. New York: Columbia University Press.

_____ (1951). Current trends in group psychotherapy. *International Journal of Group Psychotherapy* 1:7–15.

_____ (1953). Sources of countertransference and group-induced anxiety. *International Journal of Group Psychotherapy* 3:373–388.

_____ (1955). Criteria for selection and rejection of patients for various types of group psychotherapy. *International Journal of Group Psychotherapy* 5:3–30.

———— (1956). The nature and treatment of acting out in group psychotherapy. *International Journal of Group Psychotherapy* 6:3–27.

———— (1957). Are there group dynamics in therapy groups? *International Journal of Group Psychotherapy* 7:131–154.

———— (1959). A bioquantum theory of the ego. *International Journal of Group Psychotherapy* 9:3–30.

———— (1964). *A Textbook in Analytic Group Psychotherapy.* New York: International Universities Press.

Spanjaard, J. (1959). Transference neurosis and psychoanalytic group psychotherapy. *International Journal of Group Psychotherapy* 9:31–42.

Spotnitz, H. (1947). Observations on emotional currents in interview group therapy with adolescent girls. *Journal of Nervous and Mental Diseases* 106:565–582.

———— (1952a). A psychoanalytic view of resistance in groups. *International Journal of Group Psychotherapy* 2:3–9.

———— (1952b). Group therapy as a specialized technique. In *Specialized Techniques in Psychotherapy*, ed. G. Bychowski and J. L. Despert, pp. 85–101. New York: Basic Books.

———— (1957). The borderline schizophrenic in group psychotherapy. *International Journal of Group Psychotherapy* 7:155–174.

———— (1961a). The application of group psychotherapy in the treatment of the psychoneurotic syndromes. Academic lecture, Fifth Annual Institute, American Group Psychotherapy Association.

———— (1961b). *The Couch and the Circle.* New York: Alfred Knopf.

———— (1968). The management and mastery of resistance in group psychotherapy. *Journal of Group Psychoanalysis* 3:5–22.

———— (1969a). Resistance phenomena in group psychotherapy. In *Group Therapy Today: Styles, Methods and Techniques*, ed. H. Ruitenbeck, pp. 203–217. New York: Atherton Press.

———— (1969b). *Modern Psychoanalysis of the Schizophrenic Patient.* New York: Grune & Stratton.

Spotnitz, H., and Gabriel, B. (1950). Resistance in analytic group therapy: a study of the group therapeutic process in children and mothers. *Quarterly Journal of Child Behavior* 2:71–85.

Spotnitz, H., and Nagelberg, L. (1960). A preanalytic technique for resolving the narcissistic defense. *Psychiatry* 23:193–197.

Spotnitz, H., Nagelberg, L., and Feldman, Y. (1957). Ego reinforcement in the schizophrenic child. *American Journal of Orthopsychiatry* 26:146–162.

Stein, A. (1956). Group therapy with psychosomatic disorders. In *The Fields of Group Psychotherapy*, ed. S. Slavson, pp. 46–58. New York: Schocken Books.

Taylor, F. (1952). On some principles of group therapy. *British Journal of Medical Psychology* 25:128–140.

Wender, L. (1936). The dynamics of group psychotherapy and its applications. *Journal of Nervous and Mental Disease* 84:54–60.

Whitaker, D., and Lieberman, M. (1964). *Psychotherapy through the Group Process.* New York: Atherton Press.

Winnicott, D. W. (1949). Hate in the countertransference. *Journal of Psychoanalysis* 17:702–727.

Wolf, A. (1949-1950). The psychoanalysis of groups. *American Journal of Psychotherapy* 3:16-50;4:525-558.

Wolf, A., Bross, R., Flowerman, S., Greene, J., Kadis, A., et al. (1954). Sexual acting out in the psychoanalysis of groups. *International Journal of Group Psychotherapy* 4:369-380.

Wolf, A., and Schwartz, E. (1960). Psychoanalysis in groups: the mystique of group dynamics. In *Topical Problems of Psychotherapy*, vol. 2, ed. W. Hulse, pp. 119-147. Basel: S. Karger.

Yalom, I. (1970). *The Theory and Practice of Group Psychotherapy*. New York: Basic Books.

———— (1975). *The Theory and Practice of Group Psychotherapy*. 2nd ed. New York: Basic Books.

Ziferstein, I., and Grotjahn, M. (1957). Group dynamics of acting out in analytic group psychotherapy. *International Journal of Group Psychotherapy* 7:77-85.

Index